Institutional Repositories:
Content and Culture in an Open Access Environment

CHANDOS
INFORMATION PROFESSIONAL SERIES

Series Editor: Ruth Rikowski
(email: Rikowskigr@aol.com)

Chandos' new series of books are aimed at the busy information professional. They have been specially commissioned to provide the reader with an authoritative view of current thinking. They are designed to provide easy-to-read and (most importantly) practical coverage of topics that are of interest to librarians and other information professionals. If you would like a full listing of current and forthcoming titles, please visit our web site **www.chandospublishing.com** or contact Hannah Grace-Williams on email info@chandospublishing.com or telephone number +44 (0) 1865 884447.

New authors: we are always pleased to receive ideas for new titles; if you would like to write a book for Chandos, please contact Dr Glyn Jones on email gjones@chandospublishing.com or telephone number +44 (0) 1865 884447.

Bulk orders: some organisations buy a number of copies of our books. If you are interested in doing this, we would be pleased to discuss a discount. Please contact Hannah Grace-Williams on email info@chandospublishing.com or telephone number +44 (0) 1865 884447.

Institutional Repositories: Content and Culture in an Open Access Environment

CATHERINE JONES

Chandos Publishing
Oxford · England

Chandos Publishing (Oxford) Limited
Chandos House
5 & 6 Steadys Lane
Stanton Harcourt
Oxford OX29 5RL
UK
Tel: +44 (0) 1865 884447 Fax: +44 (0) 1865 884448
Email: info@chandospublishing.com
www.chandospublishing.com

First published in Great Britain in 2007

ISBN:
978 1 84334 307 3 (paperback)
978 1 84334 308 0 (hardback)
1 84334 307 X (paperback)
1 84334 308 8 (hardback)

© C. Jones, 2007

British Library Cataloguing-in-Publication Data.
A catalogue record for this book is available from the British Library.

Typeset by Domex e-Data Pvt. Ltd.
Printed in the UK and USA.

Dedicated to Michael and Aidan for their support
with my 'homework' and to Penny and Debbie for listening

Contents

List of figures and tables

Figures

Tables

About the author

Catherine Jones is Library Systems Development Manager for the Science and Technology Facilities Council (STFC) Library and Information Services, based at the Rutherford Appleton Laboratory. She is responsible for library IT strategy and policy and was the project manager for ePubs, the institutional repository of the Council for the Central Laboratory of the Research Councils (CCLRC). (STFC was formed in April 2007 from the merger of CCLRC and the Particle Physics and Research Council.) Previous roles in the library service were the Reader Services Librarian and Systems Librarian. She has worked for the library and information service for the last 13 years.

Before moving to the library service she was a database applications analyst/programmer for six years, building in-house applications to provide information management systems. She has a degree in computing and communication systems and a postgraduate qualification in information management and is a Chartered Member of CILIP. She brings both her professional library and IT skills to her current role and this book.

The author may be contacted at:

E-mail: *c.m.jones@rl.ac.uk*

Preface

This book concentrates on the policy and cultural aspects of implementing institutional repositories. As many experts in the field state, establishing the technological infrastructure is not difficult, as long as the organisation has access to the right technical support. The hard parts to repository building are deciding on the content, preservation approaches and then actually getting the content in. These are all cultural and organisational issues, which are deeply embedded within both the institution and the subject domains of the researchers. To add more difficulty to the task, the subject and institutional cultures may not be at one, and in most of those conflict situations researchers are likely to side with opinions and received wisdom in their subject area while the management of the institution try to enforce a more local viewpoint. Getting people to change is a major undertaking and this book concentrates on practical techniques. Running through this book is the theme of the stakeholders in this exercise and identifying the benefits and barriers that affect them. The stakeholders identified are not discrete groups but a complex overlapping set of people, often with conflicting attitudes depending on the role that they are performing at the time. However, the key to successful projects and services is the identification of the stakeholders and an understanding of factors motivating them.

The first five chapters of this book deal with the external environment and organisational influences on changing information access behaviours, explaining some of the reasons that institutional repositories have come into being. They look at why it is important for the library and information service within the institution to become involved with this process, and discuss the different types of content, outline issues involved in maintaining a repository, discuss work on version identification and finally consider aspects of preservation. The policy framework needed for a successful long-term implementation is discussed. To truly embed a new service into the culture of an organisation or subject discipline there needs to be benefits for all parts of the group – identifying these benefits is one of the cornerstones to success.

The sixth chapter of the book looks at three successful implementations, two based in the UK and one in New Zealand. These case studies consider various aspects of the implementation project. Comparisons and contrasts are drawn from this to provide pointers for those who are at earlier stages of the process.

There are many exciting possibilities for repositories and the resources they hold. To this end, the final chapters of this book look to the future and explore what developments might enhance the service provided by institutional repositories for their users and managers. Areas discussed include linking to experimental data, ensuring the institutional repository is linked into business processes, federating or cross-searching repositories and overlay journals. This is followed by general conclusions.

Note that where the text uses the term *author*, it does not necessarily mean that only one person is the author of the work, rather, the term is being used as shorthand for a representation of the authorship of the work. In the scientific disciplines that I am most familiar with it is rare for there to be a single author and in particle physics, in particular, there are likely to be hundreds of authors representing large multi-organisational collaborations on facilities such as the collider at CERN.

Many people have helped with this book. In particular, my thanks go to Brian Matthews, Simon Bevan, Nigel Stanger, Graham McGregor, Monica Ballantine, Simon Lambert and Keith Jeffery.

1

Introduction

This book examines the issues surrounding building, populating and maintaining institutional repositories. It is interested in the cultural aspects of repositories, and is intentionally agnostic about what software is used to create an individual repository, as all systems are trying to achieve the same ends. It intends to tie together the strategic and policy issues of building a repository to those of maintaining a digital collection over a long period. Institutional repositories are an interesting development in information provision as they demonstrate a shift from end users using centrally provided services to participating in the input to a service, somewhat mirroring the changes brought on by the community sharing software in the wider internet world.

This book is written from the perspective of a repository manager in an academic research institution. The academic institution to which I belong was, until April 2007, the Council for the Central Laboratory of the Research Councils (CCLRC) and was one of the eight UK Research Councils. This institution was unique in the Research Council family as it did not give grants to researchers but provided large-scale scientific facilities for use by academics. From April 2007, CCLRC has been merged with the Particle Physics and Astronomy Research Council to form the Science and Technology Facilities Council. This new body will both provide grants to academic researchers and large-scale scientific facilities. Before the merger, CCLRC employed 1,800 staff on three sites: Daresbury Laboratory in Cheshire, the Rutherford Appleton Laboratory in Oxfordshire and the Chilbolton Observatory in Hampshire. These sites provide facilities which include very high powered lasers and ISIS, a neutron spallation source used to examine the structure of matter. The staff provide a combination of general, scientific and technical support for the facilities and research in a wide range of sciences, from biology, through chemistry, particle physics and space science to technical innovations in computing, engineering and instrumentation. Library and information services are also provided to support both the researchers and practitioners on the three sites. The services are based on the two larger sites and employ ten members of staff, most of whom are professionally qualified. The resources offered include an extensive journals collection, books and technical reports, and resource location tools such as literature databases. While the Research Councils are very similar to the research part of the academic sector, the main difference is that they do not directly support any teaching or learning.

The CCLRC institutional repository project was managed and funded by the library and information services. As such, I make no apologies for my bias towards information professionals being strongly involved in the policy-making for, and implementation of, these new services. Research libraries are there to facilitate access to the scholarly record, and institutional repositories are intended to hold the scholarly record for a particular organisation. An underlying goal of open access is to have information freely available at the point of use, which assumes a change in publishing business models. As libraries are major customers for academic publishing, this will have a significant impact on the operation and funding of those libraries. It is in the interests of the library service to be proactively involved with all aspects of the changing information environment.

Repository definitions

The word *repository* has different meanings to different communities, while its formal definition has changed over the last 25 years. The seventh edition of the *Oxford Concise Dictionary* (1982) defines repository as a 'receptacle; place where things are stored or may be found, museum, warehouse, store, shop; burial place'. This is a useful starting point as it captures two of the most important aspects of any repository: a safe place to put something and the expectation that there will be a method of finding it again. By the 11th (revised) edition in 2006, the definition is 'a place where, or receptacle in which, things are stored; a place where something is found in significant quantities'. Here, the emphasis on quantity of content is another useful aspect to repositories in general and institutional repositories in particular, as successful repositories need a critical mass of content to justify the effort of searching it, in terms of the investment in time and learning new information location skills. In these general definitions there is no clear description of the content of the repository. In a digital context, the term 'repository' implies that, in addition to the objects themselves or the digital representation of objects, there will be information describing said objects. In this context, such information is referred to as *metadata*. There are many types of metadata but the most common is *descriptive metadata*, which is the type of information about an object that would go into a library catalogue record. Other types of metadata are described elsewhere in the text.

By using the term 'institutional repository' there is implicit narrowing of the scope to a particular type of 'thing'. There are many definitions of what this narrower term implies; for example, Raym Crow from the Scholarly Publishing and Academic Resources Coalition (SPARC) defines an institutional repository as a 'digital collection capturing and preserving the intellectual output of a single or multi-university community'.[1] This narrowing of the focus to a particular type of content (intellectual) and the organisational location of the author is what separates most institutional repositories from other similar systems. The intellectual work can take many forms but includes journal articles, books and book chapters, theses, patents, technical reports, conference materials, works of art, photographs, video recordings, data resulting from research projects and learning and teaching materials. Depending on the policies of the organisation and the needs of the producers and users of the material, all these types of material could be held in a single repository; however, it is more likely that some of the dissimilar material will be held in specialist repositories in order that the correct metadata for resource location and discovery is created and available for use. By using the term 'institutional repository' it is tempting to consider the organisation as a homogeneous unit which has the same needs regardless of the type of material or its uses; this is certainly not true, and all the needs of the stakeholder groups and the descriptive information about the material needs to be taken into consideration when deciding on the scope of the content.

Some examples of academic and related material repositories which have distinct needs are electronic document and record management systems (EDRMS); learning object repositories; collections of exam paper questions; and research data. EDRMS are used to formalise and automate organisations' document and record-keeping functions, thereby replicating paper-based archive and document registry functions. The emphasis is on keeping, and removing as appropriate, the organisation's corporate record so that decision making rather than intellectual output can be traced; to this end, little content is likely to fall into the remit of both repositories. The overlap between learning object repositories (LORs) and institutional repositories is more blurred but the main distinction is in the audience; LORs are inward-facing while many of the benefits that institutional repositories bring are external-facing. This is also true of exam paper repositories as they are by their nature not open to the general public in the same way that institutional repositories are implicitly expected to be. Research data, both from small and large-scale science has specialist needs for metadata description, which differ from experiment to experiment and in many cases additional user access requirements; consequently, these are better handled in specialised repositories.

Looking at other similar fields in the information world, it is useful to compare the different factors that have driven the institutional repository field compared with the digital library field. The Digital Library Federation uses the following working definition of a digital library:

> Digital libraries are organizations that provide the resources, including the specialized staff, to select, structure, offer intellectual access to, interpret, distribute, preserve the integrity of, and ensure the persistence over time of collections of digital works so that they are readily and economically available for use by a defined community or set of communities.[2]

Overlaps in concepts can be identified when comparing the definitions of an institutional repository and a digital library; for example, they both represent a collection of works where the content has identifiable links that add value to the whole. This common concept of 'collection' means that the skills utilised in libraries for managing the print collection can be transferred and improved to do the same for digital objects. The major differences between these types of repository can be identified as the expectation of who will be populating the system and the scope and purpose of the collection. Institutional repositories would ideally have the author themselves enter the information about their scholarly work into the system, as it is in their interests to disseminate it as widely as possible, even though they may have no interest in adding their work to a wider structured collection with internal consistency rules. For digital libraries information is likely to be added by specialist cataloguers with a professional interest in accurately and consistently describing works to aid retrieval. These different expectations alter the input dynamics and influence the quality and validation of the data within the systems.

In an institutional repository, the collection remit is based on the location and/or employer of the author whereas the collection(s) in a digital library are based on a topic or material type regardless of the location of the author, unless of course an author is a subject of a topic. The collection remit in an institutional repository should therefore be more straightforward and easily identifiable. However, institutions are not static within time and bring their own identity problems, as ably demonstrated by my own orgnisation.

One of the implicit assumptions that comes with using the term 'institutional repository' to describe a collection of institutionally related works is that, wherever legally possible, the content will be freely accessible. One of the reasons for this assumption is the importance of the concept of open access to scholarly work and the associated debate regarding the development movement for this type of repository. The concept of open access holds that the outputs of publicly-funded research should be freely available at the point of use and that one way of achieving this is to deposit the full text of the work to a publicly accessible repository. The result of doing so aids information flow between researchers. This concept and technical implementation has had two effects on the information environment: changing the expectation of the information flow between researcher and organisation, and influencing the type of technology choices made by the suppliers of the underlying software – most of which is open source and thus freely available. The open access debate does not necessarily define who should be running the publicly accessible repository. There are two options: a subject-based repository, where the collection is linked by topic, although there may be issues surrounding how this is resourced and supported, or an institutional repository, where the collection is linked to the organisation and is therefore resourced and supported by that organisation. This book addresses the issues surrounding a repository for an institution, although there is much overlap in policy between the two. An effective repository will not only have the bibliographic reference to the work in question, but wherever possible the actual digital work publicly accessible.

Although this book is about institutional repositories, a large amount of the freely available full text at present is held in subject-based repositories such as arXiv (*http://arxiv.org/*) for particle physics and PubMedCentral (*http://www.pubmedcentral.nih.gov/*) and PubMedUK (*http://ukpmc.ac.uk/*) for the biomedical sciences. These have been developed by sections of specialist communities for their community. As these disciplines can be narrowly defined and are on the whole used to working in collaborative projects they have been very successful. As they take a discipline-based approach, the information location for a potential user is straightforward as it is all in one place. The problems with this approach are the funding and long-term preservation of the repository and internal organisational issues. As the repository is for a subject area, mechanisms are needed to ensure that the infrastructure and data remain available and accessible – this is harder than for repositories based within an institution as it inevitably involves cross-organisational cooperation. To expand on the second point, most institutions are required to report on performance to justify funding decisions and having their researchers deposit material in a subject-based repository means that the information may need to be collected again.

Repositories use technological mechanisms to achieve the same subject-based functionality. A mechanism for achieving cross-searching repositories is the use and availability of the Open Archives Initiative – Protocol for Metadata Harvesting (OAI-PMH).[3] This standard allows repositories to define sets of metadata records which are visible to the protocol and can be collected automatically by other services using the protocol. This enables other services to collect the records; the technical term for this is *harvesting*. These records, together with those from other repositories can be used in services, such as a cross-searching tool, enhancing information-sharing and providing opportunities for third-party services. A good and early example of this is OAIster (*http://www.oaister.org/*), which is a system for cross-searching OAI-PMH repositories. The output format for OAI-PMH is based on the Dublin Core (DC) metadata standard. DC is a standard set of bibliographic descriptors used in the digital world; the basic profile describes 18 descriptive fields and can be ambiguous.

The DC description set is being expanded by the development of application profiles which give more detailed guidance for particular material types. These can be likened to cataloguing rules in a traditional library catalogue. The type of automatic searching enabled by OAI-PMH is not a new idea in the library world – its purpose is very similar to the Z39.50 standard for information retrieval,[4] which enables searching of other library catalogues using the searching interface of one's own catalogue regardless of the system used by the remote sites, and is proof that regardless of which particular technology is used to achieve cross-searching, this functionality is a crucial part of an information infrastructure to ensure that each individual system, whether an institutional repository or another information resource, does not become an isolated silo of knowledge. The cross-searching facility is particularly important for institutional repositories as the searching for information within repositories is predicated on the fact that the collection is linked to a particular organisation and this does not mimic traditional search strategies.

The above discussion about how to search for information leads on to the most important aspect of any repository – gaining the content. As mentioned previously, one of the ideals of open access and institutional repositories is that the creator of the work chooses to deposit it in their institutional repository, together with associated metadata for retrieval. This is much easier to write than to achieve. As open access repositories are a new phenomenon, the issue of changing author behaviour must be addressed to get successful deposition. Many academics view depositing their work in a repository as an administrative function, rather than performing a task which might have been done in other systems by a professionally trained librarian. Unfortunately for advocacy, the benefits of the deposit come to the author over the longer term as more people have access to the knowledge. Linked to this change is the wider potential change in the publishing world and the effect this may have on their academic career. If an academic is asked to peer-review articles/conference presentations then this is recognition of their abilities; changing the publishing paradigm jeopardises this relationship. There is a complex web of stakeholders in the institutional repository and these are identified and discussed throughout this book.

There is much discussion in this book about *culture*. One of the definitions of this word in the *Concise Oxford Dictionary* (7th edition) is '...particular form, stage or type of intellectual development or civilisation, group of products or achievements resulting from this'. The culture of a particular organisation is not one homogenous mass, but is a set of shared beliefs and values. This can lead to different parts of the organisation interpreting and demonstrating these communal understandings in subtly different ways. Each subject discipline also has associated cultural assumptions, and a particular academic will embed parts of these, and other influences, into their world view. Being able to understand and interpret these cultural nuances will help ensure that the best case for the benefits of an institutional repository is made according to the audience being addressed.

To expand on my personal experiences, although my organisation calls ePubs our *institutional* repository, the intention is for it to represent the scientific and technical work of the constituent laboratories. This widens the remit from just the staff of the organisation to include bibliographic information (descriptive metadata) on articles written by authors from other institutions who have used our scientific facilities to run their experiments and produce data. In these cases we do not intend to require the full text to be deposited as there may be copyright restrictions. At present we expect that these metadata records will be generated either by an internal departmental coordinator or even the experimental scientist themselves; perhaps in the future these could be automatically harvested from the institution of the experimenter. This additional criterion means that ePubs has a unique perspective, as it is midway between a repository for one institution and a subject repository. As of April 2007 there are 22,850 records, of which 800 have full-text content. It is integrated into business processes within the organisation and is being used to produce departmental bibliographies for use in annual reports and web pages, personal publication lists, and is being tested to produce some of the performance metrics for the Office of Science and Innovation, which is our parent body. Our library and information services are committed to continue to support and develop ePubs. One of the obvious effects of this is the adjustment of staffing duties to enable information professionals to quality-check the deposited records within the repository as we are aware that the contents are very visible and reflect on our reputation in the communities to which we belong. Furthermore, by using professional skills in this area the library and information service adds value to the information within the repository.

To return to the definition of repository which started this section, I was struck by the possible meaning of repository as a burial place. This inadvertently highlights an important issue for repositories, in that they should be a window onto a successful organisation, reflecting the vibrant intellectual life being undertaken there and not a place to put things to forget about and not use. To ensure that the institutional repository is a living system, cultural organisational and subject discipline issues and barriers need to be identified and addressed.

Notes

1. Crow, R. (2002) 'The case for institutional repositories: a SPARC position paper', Washington, DC: SPARC, available at: *http://www.arl.org/sparc/bm~doc/ir_final_release_102.pdf* (accessed 11 April 2007).
2. Digital Libraries Federation (1998) 'A working definition of a digital library', available at: *http://www.diglib.org/about/dldefinition.htm* (accessed 11 April 2007).
3. OAI-PMH (2004) 'The Open Archives Initiative Protocol for Metadata Harvesting', available at: *http://www.openarchives.org/OAI/openarchivesprotocol.html* (accessed 11 April 2007).
4. Library of Congress (2006) 'Information Retrieval (Z39.50) Application Service Definition and Protocol Specification', available at: *http://www.loc.gov/z3950/agency/* (accessed 11 April 2007).

2

The changing information environment

Introduction

While the issues discussed in this chapter relate to all types of information, the focus is material of academic interest, relating to learning, teaching and research.

Over the last 40 years, information provision has changed and adapted through effective use of computers and technology. Computers have revolutionised information storage and retrieval. In the library domain, information retrieval routes using resources such as card catalogues with preset indices and printed paper abstracts from third-party aggregators have been swept away by library management systems with their associated online catalogues and abstract and indexing databases, where the metadata in bibliographic records can be used to locate the required information. This has been further developed with digital library systems that provide digital access to the object. The same changes have affected publishing, making the production of the written word easier and opening access to the pre-publication stages more widely than before. This chapter identifies particular issues arising from these changes – from information silos to information freely accessible using search engines. It starts by identifying stakeholders and their viewpoints.

Identifying stakeholders

To be able to influence the decision makers and the potential users of the repository, it is first useful to identify them and their particular viewpoints. In this environment, stakeholders can be grouped into four broad categories: users of information (end users), information providers, information mediators and users of meta-information (information about information). The first three groups are concerned with different aspects of intellectual content provision, the last is interested in the impact of the process rather than the outcomes. A particular person may be in more than one group depending on their role and responsibilities, but each role may have different perspectives on the same issues.

End users of information

End users are defined as the group of people who need access to the contents of academic material to support their research, teaching or learning. These users are likely to have a strong sense of belonging to a subject-based community with a set of expectations of the type of material that will satisfy their requirements. They must be able to identify, locate and read relevant information. In this context, end-users are a collection of individuals, not corporate entities.

There are many types of information. Some of the most common ones include journal articles, monographs, working papers, technical reports, experimental data and unpublished material. The relative importance and use of each type of material is very discipline-based and there are very different viewpoints on how formally the information needs to have been published depending on the discipline. For some disciplines, especially in the science, technology and medicine sector, the information has to be electronically available and accessible from the desktop, regardless of the age of the material.

End users in a particular subject area should not be considered as a homogeneous group, as they all have their own different information needs and preferences. Some of this may be set by personal learning styles, but experience of information seeking will affect the methods used to retrieve relevant material.

In an institutional repository context, the bulk of end users of the content will be external to the organisation, while the community supported will be end users of other repositories.

Information providers

This group consists of both individuals and corporate entities. The common theme is the dissemination of information, either by producing it or providing the mechanisms to provide access to it. This is an area with a lot of symbiosis, as authors depend on a publishing mechanism as the main dissemination method, publishers depend on people and organisations buying the material, and organisations, usually through their library, depend on the material being available and of sufficient quality to be useful for their user communities. These constituent parts are now considered in turn.

Authors

The entire publishing paradigm is based on having authors. They produce their written output to disseminate the results of their research or project. This formal mechanism then drives career progression and is hugely influential in determining attitudes to dissemination. In an academic environment, the amount and 'quality' of publishing that one does reflects on one's career; many established authors may therefore be resistant to changes in the publishing paradigm. The subject area and its culture is an important factor in influencing attitudes to publishing and suitable avenues for dissemination. Most authors are aligned to institutions which provide them with resources – this will also affect their attitudes to publishing. To be able to produce high-quality intellectual output, the author needs to be an end-user to gather information on the subject area.

Many authors are not fully aware of the complex issues surrounding designation of copyright when publishing scholarly works and may sign over rights that they may wish to retain, or even rights that they do not own depending on their relationship with their employer or funder.

Authors of short pieces of work, such as journal articles or conference papers, typically do not receive any direct financial recompense for the work involved in producing the material; larger works, such as books, will have some personal recompense attached to them. However, in scholarly circles the most important rewards are gained through the recognition involved; financial recompense is provided by the employer through a salary, with the expectation that the job entails producing scholarly communications.

This complex entanglement of personal recognition through intellectual work that has no direct financial effect on the author, together with the costs to the organisation of purchasing the content the authors need to be able to produce is a difficult matter to balance.

In an institutional repository context, authors are very important as they are responsible for generating the content of the system. One of the hardest issues to overcome is to influence and persuade this group of people to change their attitudes and behaviour to enable the repository to hold this content.

Peer reviewers

These individuals are recognised experts within their domain and contribute to the dissemination field by peer reviewing material, typically journal articles or conference papers. The peer-review process is designed to ensure that the intellectual content of the material is checked for validity. They provide their services free of charge but gain recognition within their domain for their expertise.

As publication is the major process by which expertise in a subject is recognised, peer reviewers will also be authors. To this end, they will have an interest in the way that the publication process operates.

Publishers

Publishers are the organisations that take the written intellectual output from an author and transform it into an information commodity which is acquired by, or on behalf of, end users. The term 'publisher' covers a wide range of organisations, with a range of reasons for undertaking the publishing process, from those who wish to make it a commercial concern, to those who are supporting a particular community, such as learned societies or a user group, to organisations disseminating their outputs through grey literature. Using the term 'publisher' does not imply that the material is to be paid for at the end of the process, but in many cases this is true. For some publishers, such as learned societies, the profits support work for their subject-based community in other ways.

The publishing process adds value by providing a quality assurance mechanism; professional editing of the copy to make it more readable, publicity for the work, and a mechanism for disseminating the work, either through a website for electronic information or through print. For some types of material, such as journal articles, publishers package relevant and like-minded pieces of work together into journal titles, providing an easier location mechanism for the information. In return for providing the publication process, some of the author's rights in the material are transferred to the publisher. Exactly which rights these include depends on the publisher.

These enhanced resources are then supplied to the relevant user communities, in most cases through the mediation of an institutional library and information service. The publication may be accessed following some financial transaction or, in the case of open access journals, may be free at the point of use.

In the traditional print world, the publisher will maintain copies of the material that they have published, but they do not have an explicit preservation role. In the electronic world, where the model has changed from ownership to access, this preservation role has become more important.

In an institutional repository context, a publisher's commitment to open access publishing will dictate their position as to the type of content they would like to see held by repositories. Their business is deeply affected by the potential changes in the publishing paradigm.

Library and information services

Organisations that support research, teaching and learning need to give access to the information commodities required by these people. This is usually done by providing a library or information service. The role of the library and information service is to select resources at the appropriate level(s) for their user communities and to use their skills to provide access in the most appropriate manner within the budget allocated by the organisation.

As electronic resources have become more commonplace, the role played by a library service in ensuring authorisation and authentication to resources has become more complicated. In addition, more 'definite' statistics are now available, leading to more management accounting. Whether this is more accurate than what went before is difficult to interpret, as it is not always possible to compare across publishers, although there is research into standards in this area. There is also the issue of maintaining the intellectual record of the organisation.

As libraries are the main consumers of academic publishing, changes to the paradigm will impact on the service provided and the resourcing and skill sets of the people employed by the library service. While it is a great opportunity for greater access to information, it is also a threat to the funding of the service.

In an institutional repository context, it is likely that the expertise of library staff will be recognised and used to ensure that the content is verified and validated. The expertise about publications and the nuances of describing them effectively are essential if long-term preservation is to be achieved. The role of the library service within the organisation, providing information resources to all, means that it is an ideal location for repository management.

National libraries

These typically have a remit to preserve their nation's intellectual heritage in perpetuity, but often provide last resort lending services for other libraries if the material is not held locally. They can also be used by end users directly.

The explosion in publishing and the changes in media have influenced strategic direction. The issues surrounding collecting electronic material and preserving it in perpetuity are more complex and less well known than in the print world. Decisions over strategic direction affect the library communities they support.

It is difficult to gauge the effects of the changes in publishing and the impacts of institutional repositories on national libraries.

Information mediators

These organisations or individuals contribute to the provision of content by providing alternative location methods. They are not actually responsible for the creation or distribution of the content.

Aggregators and abstracting services

Such organisations overlay specific publishers to provide information resources at a higher level than aggregation at a specific subject level, such as provided by journal title. These information resources are now usually provided in electronic form and give access to information on content within certain domain or material types. These are used by end users as a location tool for content which they have not yet discovered but believe is available. Most of these tools do not have full-text content but point to the content in other material forms. They may add additional value through analysis of the information to provide services such as citation indices. Examples of this type of service include ISI's Web of Knowledge (*http://isiwebofknowledge.com/*), which abstracts journal articles and conference proceedings across a wide range of subject areas. As many of these are paid services they are often mediated through the institution's library and information service.

This type of service, which collects information from many dissemination sources and provides a common location interface, usually with some subject access points, will be needed in an information landscape full of repositories; whether this is done by the same organisations as at present, is difficult to forecast.

Search engines

Following developments such as Google Scholar (*http:// scholar.google.com/*) and changes in the ways publishers make their journals available electronically, general purpose search engines, designed to locate any resource on the internet, are often the starting point for many readers when trying to locate 'scholarly' work.

The development of open accessible content from institutional repositories has widened the potential results for search engines.

Meta-information users

This group of organisations is more interested in using information about the content, rather than the content itself, for internal management processes. These organisations have a great influence as they tend to have sufficient budget to support research, teaching and learning. This group is also likely to have a wider perspective on the issues involved in this area as their core business does not revolve around information provision and dissemination.

Funders

These provide financial support to institutions, projects and programmes to broaden knowledge in particular domains and there is an expectation that the results will be disseminated through public mechanisms so that the full benefits of the research reaches the community for which it is intended. It can be difficult for a funder to assess the publishing success of a particular programme due to the inherent problems in collecting this information. The usual practice is for the author to acknowledge the funder in the text; this means that it is impossible to use aggregators' systems to find publications by funder. An alternative mechanism is to require the individual or organisation receiving funding to provide a bibliography of publications resulting from it. However, this presents the problem of getting the information from a third party, usually after the funds have been handed over, and is also staff-intensive.

Institutional and subject-based repositories are more aware of the funding issues, and it may be possible to locate this information as a result. In certain fields, funders are requiring those who receive money to deposit in a defined repository as part of the funding process. Within this context, this can result in tension between the external funding sources and the institution itself.

Institutions

In this context, 'institutions' is taken to mean the body which financially supports authors, readers and library and information services, and would be the body which would brand the repository. The organisation's academic performance can be measured by levels and quality of research output and the publishing sphere is a strong component of this at present. The overall academic performance is important as it can affect the external funding and the quality of potential staff and students.

It is likely that institutions, or component parts, have collected information on intellectual outputs to be able to measure performance at many different levels, such as the individual staff member, for personal performance and reward, or department, for funding or strategic reasons. The institutional repository gives a focus to this information gathering and will increase visibility in the wider world.

National bodies

While national bodies such as the UK's Joint Information Steering Committee (JISC), whose mission is to 'provide world-class leadership in the innovative use of Information and Communications Technology to support education and research'[1] may not be directly involved with day-to-day information provision, they have remits to influence the wider information landscape. JISC, for example, can affect the academic information landscape in three major ways: by promoting a view of the information landscape called the 'information environment', by work through JISC Collections on journal deals for the community, and by funding IT projects, especially in this context in the digital repository area.

These bodies may have a view on institutional repositories and can influence other stakeholders by making national policy or providing leadership.

All these different stakeholder groups have views and influence the way institutions respond to the changing information environment. It is important to recognise their different needs when planning for future developments.

The changing journals environment

For many academic disciplines the peer-reviewed journal is the bedrock of the formal record. For academics to progress in their careers they must write papers in high-quality journals. As their careers continue they are likely to become peer-reviewers in their field and some will be editors of journals. Journals are intimately bound up with academic careers for some disciplines, but not all. This makes changes to the publishing paradigm more high profile than changes in other material type areas.

The production and distribution of journals have undergone the most change where advances in technology and the format of the material being provided have given the greatest opportunities for expanding information provision. One such high impact factor is the change to an electronic delivery mechanism. For some titles this is achieved by producing an electronic version of the print original, in other cases the title is only available electronically. Most journals in the science, technology and medicine (STM) sector have electronic services and the number of electronic-only titles is steadily rising.

These electronic journals have many benefits to end-user stakeholders as outlined below:

- They are the preferred delivery mechanism for most academic users. The information required is accessible from their working environment without physically having to go to the library building.

- Electronic versions are able to link to simulations, graphics and even the underlying data, thus exploiting capabilities that the print medium cannot offer.

- For print titles, issues need to be physically distributed from the printer to the reader; for titles published overseas this could take weeks and this delay is therefore apparent to the subscriber. In delivering the article to the desktop, electronic access has accelerated, or in some cases abolished, the access lead time to publications. This has obvious benefits to the readers of the material.

- Electronic access extends beyond the period that the technology has been available. The medium has been so popular that many publishers have invested in digitising their entire back catalogues of journal titles to increase access, usage and leverage value on existing outputs.

- Electronic access has reduced barriers by allowing for multiple concurrent use of the same subscription so the journal is always available for the end user regardless of how many other people are reading it.

There are a few disadvantages to electronic titles for readers, the prime one being that it is difficult to replicate the serendipitous discovery of useful articles by browsing a physical journal issue. There are of course readers who prefer to see the articles in print and like the physical sensation of reading a journal issue.

Although electronic publication has improved access to information for those readers associated with organisations that subscribe to the titles they wish to read, it has led to a more complex environment for libraries. In a print world, organisational access to information was simpler. If the title was of high importance to the organisation's business then a subscription to the print journal was started and physical resources (staff, shelving, buildings etc.) were provided to support long-term access. If the title was less significant, then it was subscribed to and disposed of once no longer useful or document delivery services provided by other libraries were used. The people who were allowed to use the institutional subscriptions were limited to those who were allowed to enter the physical library. If the title stopped, or it was no longer purchased, access was retained automatically while the title remained physically on library shelves. Collection usage would be monitored for the journal title and collection retention decisions would be made, recognising that it is difficult to track print collection usage. These straightforward rules and assumptions do not work in the electronic world as it is rare to actually hold the electronic version locally. This means that the organisational attitudes to information have altered as the paradigm from ownership to access has taken hold. The benefits to organisations and their libraries can be summarised below:

- Multi-site licences have reduced the need for duplication for libraries with more than one site. This has widened the potential usage of each subscription.

- Statistics are easy to produce and with the standardisation work of Counting Online Usage of NeTworked Electronic Resources (COUNTER) it is possible to compare across journal providers and publishers (*http:// www.projectcounter.org/*). COUNTER is a not for profit company which aims to provide an agreed set of standards and protocols so that usage data can be recorded and exchanged. At present this work covers journals, databases, books and reference works. These standards are produced and ratified by a wide range of stakeholders in this process including publishers, libraries and intermediaries. These standards are important as they mean that statistics from different producers can be compared, secure in the knowledge that the semantics are the same.

- Electronic back catalogues have meant that retention schedules can be examined to see if the print version is still required, thus releasing space in the physical environment.

- The technique of bundling or big deals has widened the number of titles to which libraries can give access.

However, there are some less positive changes for libraries:

- The licence restrictions mean that there are limitations on who can use the material. This is a particularly complex area. In the print world, a library could allow anyone who was entitled to enter the building to use their journal collection. In the electronic world, especially for libraries using academic licences, then the status of the person is important, for example, whether commercial or not. As many research and teaching organisations start to have more complex arrangements with business it is often unclear where the boundaries of commerce versus academia lie. To complicate matters, different publishers have different licences so that it is not possible to have a single straightforward access policy.

- The medium makes it difficult to ensure that the title is accessible and has led to a new collection of access issues beyond the journal being 'lost in the post'. An obvious issue is translating the print journal concept of processing new issues into an equivalent electronic process. In the print world it is obvious when an issue has not arrived and there are standard procedures for alerting the publisher that the subscription has not been fulfilled. In this case the status information is being 'pushed' to the library; in the electronic world the reverse is true and the status information has to be 'pulled' from the provider. There is no notification process to see if the new electronic issue has been made available, apart from alerting services designed for current awareness for the end user. Thus, to achieve the same effect as print, librarians would have to check each title. This is very labour-intensive and on the whole has not been adopted. Instead libraries have used technology or user feedback to track availability problems. The technology has included URL link checkers to find broken links and the adoption of the OpenURL standard[2] and link resolvers. Another accessibility issue occurs at subscription renewal time where access can be denied if there are problems ensuring the payment has been processed by all involved.

- Access to the full subscription period may become unavailable if the title is cancelled by the publisher. This models the database subscription world where access ceases once it is not being paid for. However, access to the issues that have been paid for is retained in a journals print model for as long as the print version is available.

- Bundling may provide access to titles that are less relevant to the collection. Subsequently there is a management decision about what to do with these additional titles.

- As electronic journals have shifted the paradigm from ownership of print to access to electronic resources typically located on the provider's equipment, preservation and perpetual access to the information that has been purchased is outside the remit of the library with the subscription. The problem of long-term access to the electronic version also holds in cases where the publisher ceases to do business and no one is responsible for keeping the electronic archive available.

There have been many technical developments focused on reducing the negative changes for library services and some of these are discussed in the following section.

Persistent identification of electronic articles is addressed by the Digital Object Identifier (DOI) service provided by CrossRef (*http://www.crossref.org/*). The DOI should always locate the same article regardless of any underlying infrastructure changes.

Electronic access has made locating full-text content more difficult as access is no longer through a physical copy on a library shelf but through an electronic interface which may be provided by a variety of methods, such as a publisher's website, a journal aggregator or a subscription agent etc. The same content may be available through a variety of interfaces, so it becomes difficult to point the end user to the preferred access method. The OpenURL standard and associated OpenURL link resolvers provide a solution both to aiding end users locate the appropriate copy and to ensuring the correct URL is used. The standard defines a way of using logic to describe how a URL to a particular journal article is constructed so that it can be generated dynamically and link resolver software can use it to provide access services. There are usually two parts to this system, the first is a knowledge base which holds the information on the logic and syntax for creating each journal title's URL, together with the institution's subscription information. The second part defines how the link resolver is to operate and what options will be available to the users of the service. The knowledge base is updated by the supplier on a regular basis, ensuring that any changes to the link logic or underlying infrastructure are recorded as soon as possible, reducing the chances of broken links. A link resolver can be used in two ways. End users can either use the software directly, perhaps from an A–Z list of subscribed journals, or via third-party software, such as journal article databases. In the latter case, when the result set is shown, there is an option to check the end user's institutional link resolver, which will provide a menu of options as to how to get hold of the full text. The options are defined by the library service and usually include the full text if available. If the full text is not available, the end user might be offered a search in the local library catalogue, an interlibrary loan form, or access to a document delivery service. As institutional repositories become major players in the information landscape, they represent further options, assuming they are OpenURL enabled. This technology links the electronic content to the resource location tool in a seamless fashion, thereby overcoming any access barriers to the information.

Another major change is the availability of services, from journal publishers and aggregators, providing on-demand access to individual articles as an alternative to the journal subscription model. These services provide electronic copies to the desktop and are an appealing solution to some information needs, representing an alternative to document supply from another library service. However, such services tend to be more expensive in the UK than library-to-library document supply as a copyright fee is payable.

Regarding preservation and access to electronic material, a major development to ensure perpetual access to titles that may cease is the Lots Of Copies Keeps Stuff Safe programme (LOCKSS; *http://www.lockss.org/*). As suggested by the name, this programme uses the principle of maintaining multiple copies of the journals in different locations to ensure that they are preserved correctly. An organisation with a LOCKSS server maintains copies of the electronic content to which it subscribes and, on a regular basis, checks this content against other people's copies to discover whether it has become corrupted. They, and the other participating organisations, are only allowed to use this local version if the publisher site is no longer operational. The LOCKSS consortium has negotiated with the participating publishers to ensure that they have the legal right to hold this information.

Another approach is taken by Portico (*http://www.portico.org/*), which also aims to preserve electronic journals. The source files from the journal publishers are taken and migrated to an archival format. This format will be kept under supervision and the files migrated as obsolescence becomes an issue.

The changes in publishing technology have also led to an explosion in the titles available. While there are still many old and respected journals, there is also a wide variety to choose from in newer subjects. This leads to budgeting problems at the library service level for titles that use the subscription paradigm, as most organisations have fixed budgets and subscribing to new titles requires cancelling lesser used ones. The new open access journal model, where the payment is made at article submission and the article is freely available, is a growing field that transfers the responsibility for payment if the organisation both produces and consumes journal article information. The budget implications of journals subscriptions represent a major issue for libraries. Subscriptions generally cost substantial amounts of money, with each title effectively in a monopoly position. Year on year price rises averaging around 7–10 per cent lead to problems with budgets, which do not tend to rise above inflation. These price pressures can be seen by the data provided by EBSCO, a subscription agent.[3] The pressures that this brings represent one of the contributing factors to the rise in institutional interest in repositories.

Open access

Open access is the concept of making publicly-funded research freely available to all at the point of use. This is a change from traditional academic publishing where there is a subscription charge before the item, usually a journal article in this context, is available. There are two models for achieving this aim, both of which rely on having publicly accessible repositories available in which authors can deposit their work; these can be subject or institutionally based. This section outlines the background to the movement, the alternatives for achieving this aim and the present situation.

There have been three influential meetings which have progressed this concept of open access. The first was in Budapest, Hungary in December 2001,[4] the second in Bethesda, USA in April 2003[5] and the third was in Berlin, Germany in October 2003.[6] These are each examined in turn below.

The Budapest Open Access Initiative

The meeting brought together a small set of interested parties to discuss how literature which is provided freely by authors can be disseminated freely to end users. The meeting identified two strategies to achieving the long-term goal:

- *self-archiving*: depositing a copy of the peer-reviewed article in an open repository;

- *open access journals*: these will be funded by other means rather than subscription and will encompass both new and existing journals making the articles freely available to the end user.

The Bethesda Statement on Open Access Publishing

The meeting brought together interested parties in the biomedical subject area to discuss how progress could be made in achieving the goal of freely available academic literature. These parties included publishers, librarians and funding organisations. The resulting statement defined two criteria for publications to be considered to be open access:

- rights to access and use the material are granted to users in perpetuity by the copyright holders;

- a complete version of the work is submitted to an appropriate repository which is committed to long-term archiving.

The meeting had three working groups which also made statements:

- *Institutions and funding agencies* encouraged the authors they supported financially to adopt the principles of open access publishing, acknowledged that there would be financial implications, reaffirmed that the quality of the work was the most important factor in publishing, and stated they would consider open access publishing when looking at appointments or grant applications.

- *Libraries and publishers* acknowledged that there would be disruption as the publishing paradigm altered. The libraries proposed to support the transition, publicise the benefits and to highlight open access journals. The publishers committed to providing open access options, declaring a timetable for the change, working with others to achieve standard formats for archiving and ensuring that developing countries were not disadvantaged by the change.

- *Scientists and scientific societies* endorsed the principles, highlighted the importance of the publishing process, and committed to using and educating others about the benefits of open access and reflecting this in appointments and tenure.

These statements encapsulate the different issues and viewpoints in the open access debate. This meeting was followed six months later by the Conference on Open Access to Knowledge in the Sciences and Humanities which was held in Berlin, Germany.

The Berlin Declaration on Open Access to Knowledge in the Sciences and Humanities

This meeting set out to suggest measures to promote the internet as an instrument for providing and maintaining the academic knowledge base within an open access context. Their definition of an 'open access contribution' went further than papers and included original scientific results and digital representations of pictures etc. Two conditions were put forward: first, that there be no restrictive licences or copyright assigned, and second, that the content be in at least one publicly accessible repository.

To achieve this, a variety of activities are required, including encouraging funders to mandate the conditions, ensuring quality assurance in the new open access publishing world, advocating that open access publication should be included in assessment of academic merit, and encouraging the building of an open access infrastructure.

Institutions were encouraged to sign up to the Berlin Declaration and as of June 2007, some 233 organisations worldwide have done so.

There have been annual follow-up meetings to continue this and a roadmap to open access has been produced to aid implementation. The key actions that institutions should take are to implement a policy requiring authors to deposit a copy in a repository and to encourage users to publish in open access journals.

Overview of models to achieve this

Achieving open access will involve a change in paradigm from subscription-based business models to other means. There are presently two models which may achieve the goal, commonly known as the gold and green routes.

Gold

With the gold route, the paper is published in a journal which is free at the point of use. As there are costs involved with journal production, the payment has to be transferred to another point in the cycle. There are two common methods: either the journal is subsidised by interested parties or the author pays a fee when the paper is submitted for publication. In an ideal world the institution or project that is supporting the research has a dissemination budget to ensure that open access titles can be used. There are growing numbers of these and the Directory of Open Access Journals (*http://www.doaj.org/*) is a good source of information about them. Many traditional publishers are trialling dual funding of subscription titles. This allows the author to decide whether to pay and make the article open access, or to publish in the traditional method. In addition, the author deposits the article in a suitable institutional or subject-based repository.

The most commonly perceived disadvantage to this model is that income is directly related to acceptance rates. To this end, there might be a temptation to lower rejection rates in return for a higher income. However, this would also mean that the quality of the journal would diminish and that authors would therefore not select it in future, thus shooting the journal in the foot. There is also the problem for authors who do not have the funds to pay for submitting articles.

Green

With the green route, the paper is placed in an openly accessible repository (subject or institutional) as the primary place of publication but may also be formally published.

The most commonly discussed disadvantage to this model is that if the article is only placed in a repository then there are no formal, external quality control checks. To solve this problem, some formal quality control body (or bodies, as there are many different subjects) would have to be identified and payment mechanisms put in place.

Most publishers allow the deposition of an article into a repository, although there are differences as to whether this version is pre-publication or the final published version. Some publishers also have an embargo period, which means that there is a gap between the article being published and accessible from a repository. The SHERPA RoMEO service (*http://www.sherpa.ac.uk/romeo.php*) tracks the different publisher and journal positions on this and is an invaluable resource.

National and local guidance is necessary to change the way information is disseminated. The following is an overview of the state, as of spring 2007.

UK

The UK Research Councils provide funding for research in all subject areas. Until April 2007 there were eight Research Councils in the UK covering all subject areas. Seven of these were established to give grants and fund research programmes, while the eighth (CCLRC) was set up to provide large-scale scientific facilities primarily for the UK academic community although it is also used internationally. From April 2007 there are seven Research Councils, as CCLRC and PPARC have merged to form the Scientific and Technology Facilities Council (STFC). All Research Councils are strategically coordinated through a collective body called RCUK, which published its position statement on access to research outputs in June 2006.[7] The statement has four guiding principles:

- Ideas and knowledge derived from publicly-funded research must be made available and accessible for public use, interrogation and scrutiny, as widely, rapidly and effectively as practicable.

- Published research outputs must be subject to rigorous quality assurance, through effective peer-review mechanisms.

- The models and mechanisms for publication and access to research results must be both efficient and cost-effective in the use of public funds.

- The outputs from current and future research must be preserved and remain accessible for future generations.

As the respective Research Councils support different communities, each has individual guidance on the application of these principles. As the STFC guidance was not available at the time of writing, Table 2.1 reflects the pre-April situation.

The Wellcome Trust, an independent charity which provides funding for research to improve human and animal health, has been an early adopter of the open access principles. Its present policy supports 'unrestricted access to the published output of research as a fundamental part of its charitable mission'.[8] In pursuit of this broad aim, the Trust:

- encourages authors to make results available freely and to consider the copyright position;

Table 2.1	UK Research Council open access guidance

Research Council	Main points
Arts and Humanities Research Council	Consultation phase
Biotechnology and Biological Sciences Research Council	Mandatory deposit of paper resulting from funding in an appropriate e-print repository where one exists.
Council for the Central Laboratory of the Research Council	Strongly encourages deposit of papers resulting from use of CCLRC facilities or grants in the CCLRC institutional repository
Engineering and Physical Sciences Research Council	Awaiting results of a survey due to report in late 2008 before setting guidelines
Economic and Social Research Council	Mandatory deposit of paper resulting from funding in the ESRC awards and outputs repository; also encouraged to deposit in institutional repository
Medical Research Council	Mandatory deposit of paper resulting from funding in PubMedCentral, at the earliest opportunity; also encouraged to deposit in institutional repository. Strongly encourages authors to publish in journals which allow them to retain copyright.
Natural Environment Research Council	Mandatory deposit of paper resulting from funding in institutional repository or NERC repository if no local institutional repository available
Particle Physics and Astronomy Research Council	Grant holders to deposit in institutional repository

- supports grant holders with page charges for open access publishers;

- requires electronic copies of research funded or supported by the Trust to be deposited in PubMedCentral or PubMedUK;

- affirms that the work, rather than the journal in which it has been published, should be used in making funding decisions.

The strategic body for UK Universities (UUK) policy-statement on open access covers the following key points:[9]

- It supports the principle that the outcomes of publicly-funded research should be available with no barriers to access.

- It recognises that advances in technology and models, including repositories and open access journals present new opportunities, that a mixed economy is likely, and that the impact on learned societies should be monitored.

- It recognises that robust peer-review mechanisms are essential and agrees with the RCUK statement.

- It recognises that institutional repositories give an opportunity for universities to work together and offer clear benefits for universities.

- It believes that open access encourages authors and their institutions to be more proactive in managing research outcomes and associated intellectual property.

- It recognises that more access to research information would improve the teaching and learning environment.

- It welcomes moves by research funders to encourage open access to the research they fund.

The Joint Information Steering Committee (JISC), established to support the uptake of IT in the UK academic environment, both supports the RCUK position and is providing funding for institutional repository projects.[10]

The SHERPA OpenDOAR project (*http://www.opendoar.org/*) provides information on worldwide repositories, both institutional and subject-based. Within the UK, as of November 2006, there are 80 repositories registered in OpenDOAR, showing that these are becoming established within the academic community.

Europe

The European Commission has produced a communication on the subject of scientific information in the digital age.[11] This focuses on access, dissemination and preservation. The main actions from this are to ensure a contribution to publishing costs as part of grants, to provide funding for projects in this area, and to contribute to policy and debate. This communication covers both publications and data. An important repository project is DRIVER (*http://www.driver-repository.eu/*) which aims to build a network of European scientific repositories.

In the Netherlands, the Dutch universities developed the Digital Academic Repositories resource DAREnet (*http://www.darenet.nl/en/page/language.view/home*) in collaboration with SURF, the Dutch higher education and research organisation for network services and information and communications technology (*http://www.surf.nl/ smartsite.dws?id=5289&ch=ENG*). DAREnet enables the user to search over all the information held in the separate university repositories. It does not dictate what level of information is provided – this is left as a local decision. One of the off-shoots of DAREnet is the Cream of Science project (*http://www.creamofscience.org/en/page/language.view/keur .page*) which showcases the corpus of works of over 200 of the most prominent Dutch scientists. This has been very successful and has led to a large amount of publicity both for the scientists and the concept of repositories.

USA

The Federal Research Public Access Act 2006 makes the following provisions for publicly (federally) funded research in the USA:

- That the journal article should be deposited in a publicly accessible repository, either run by a Federal Agency or others which meet the approval of the agency.
- This should happen no later than six months after publication.
- If the publishers allow, then the published version should be accessible.

Within the USA, as of November 2006, there are 250 repositories registered in OpenDOAR.

Australia

The Department for Education, Science and Training (*http://www.dest.gov.au*) provides support for the repository programme, through its strategic accessibility framework.[12] Particular aspects being addressed are the development of a centre of excellence, work on a national collection of theses, work on middleware and software solutions to support best practice.

New Zealand

The New Zealand government's digital strategy (*http://www.digitalstrategy.govt.nz/*) addresses content, connection and confidence. Following on from this, the National Library of New Zealand set up a working party on repositories, which in turn produced a feasibility study report.[13] The main recommendations from this report were to establish a national federation to support institutional initiatives and to adopt a common roadmap. The Open Access Repositories in New Zealand (OARiNZ) project (*http://www.oarinz.ac.nz/*) is taking this forward.

Changing information seeking behaviours

The changes in the way information is provided together with other technological and social changes has led to a revolution in the way that information is located and perceived by those who need to find and use it. Table 2.2 illustrates some of the changes in technology over the last 40 years.

These changes which have been enabled through technology have led to a learning and research environment where information needs blend seamlessly with everyday needs. For example, the same information retrieval skills might be used to locate electronically a telephone number or an academic paper. Those people whose environment has always included networked computers have a more seamless attitude to information than those who have lived through these changes in information provision. The current generation of students have different expectations about what and how information is located and those who are providing the access services and information need to adapt to this shift in perceptions.

Online communities have been built using tools such as mailing list services, like JISCmail (*http://www.jiscmail.ac.uk*) in the UK, for at least a decade. However, tools for

| Table 2.2 | | Changes in information technologies and behaviours | |

Decade	General information/work environment	Information dissemination behaviour	Information seeking behaviours
1960s	Paper based Few computers Fixed line telephones only Typing pools for producing documents Music on vinyl discs	Published material in print Original likely to be typed	Information only available on paper Paper abstracts such as chemical abstracts used to locate new journal articles Online databases started
1980s	Personal computers arrive E-mail available – but not always outside the workplace Mobile phone technology arrives Networked computers at work – start of services which allow remote searching of other sites, such as gopher Typing pools becoming rare as word processing taking over Music on vinyl and tapes	Published material in print Original could be print or born-digital	Paper journals Online abstract services but mediated through librarian due to costs
2000s	Mobile phones Networked computers at work and home Advances in network technology such as wireless and broadband E-mail accounts available from third parties not just employers Internet and search engines Music on CDs and digitally downloadable	Published material likely to be available electronically first Original born-digital	Electronic journals the norm Electronic books and reference material Information sharing through wikis and blogs Internet search engines Specialist tools such as Google Scholar Shared/community sites Start of peer-to-peer services

'personal' communication have expanded over the last few years, with the opportunities provided by blogs and wikis giving an opportunity to publish/expose ideas and opinions, as well as increasing the ability of the reader to contribute back to the resource in a way that is difficult to achieve in printed form. In print, the obvious ways of responding are publicly, by writing a letter or another piece, or privately, by writing in the margins.

A well known and early example of this shift is Wikipedia (*http://www.wikipedia.org/*), which uses wiki technology to produce an encyclopaedia. This site was started in 2001 and currently has over 1,800,000 articles in English alone. Anyone may edit pages but there is a comprehensive organisation of editors and a set style guide to inform additional content. If someone enters incorrect information, maliciously or by misunderstanding, then it is identified and corrected by others in the community. By adopting this approach, Wikipedia has brought both strengths and weaknesses to information content and provision. It builds on shared values and altruism to aggregate and disseminate information. Many of the contributors are experts in their fields, but it also can introduce bias through the contributors. Wikipedia is providing the same service as a traditional encyclopaedia but in a collaborative fashion. This changes the viewpoints on how users judge relevance and correctness from some remote publisher to acknowledged experts in the field. Those experts may have written pieces in printed encyclopaedias but their personal identity is obscured by the brand of the formal work. By making all types of information readily accessible from the same point, this is diminishing the visual cues as to how reliable the information might be. Another interesting aspect to note is that in its help pages, Wikipedia reminds its users that the older the article, the more reliable the information is likely to be as consensus on the content will have been achieved. This is a difference to a print encyclopaedia and is in fact the reason why new editions of print encyclopaedias take so long to produce. Everyone who uses information makes implicit decisions about how reliable and valuable the information is; for example, something written on a scrap of paper by an unknown hand may not be as reliable as something from a printed encyclopaedia. It is important to acknowledge and understand these decisions as part of academic rigour rather than to take everything as relevant and reliable.

The next stages in collaborative work, which can be used in both formal and informal settings, are services such as the webpage bookmarking site Del.icio.us (*http://del.icio.us/*) and the digital picture sharing site Flickr (*http://www. flickr.com/*), which allow the sharing of personal resources with a wider community which is not formalised in the way that mailing lists are. Both these examples give the user, after a registration process, the ability to manage their own content or share it with others. To facilitate sharing, these services allow for the development of shared descriptive language through the concept of content 'tagging'. Tags are used by the creator to give subject references to the item to help location; if these tags are shared with the rest of the online community then an informal thesaurus or ontology is built. This is in contrast to the formal subject definitions within a thesaurus used by longstanding information resources.

Another interesting development is Second Life (*http:// www.secondlife.com/*), a virtual world in which users can interact with each other and the environment through avatars. The environment blurs reality by providing the same experiences as the real world, with developments including library and information services.

Taking the principles of openness and access to a new level, developments in peer-to-peer services allows people on a network to see and access the drives on one another's computers, enabling the sharing of content. These collaborative ventures assume a level of trust in the community and expect that everyone is working towards a common good. Using such methods also means that individuals need to decide about the quality of the information they have retrieved if it is to form part of intellectual endeavour.

Formal search techniques, such as the use of Boolean algebra or positional functions, have become less important now that search engines can access more objects' metadata or full text. There is no need to fully understand how the information is organised to perform effective retrieval. On the whole, most searchers will put one or two words into a search box and expect relevant answers on the first page of the result set. Although specialised searchers, such as librarians or subject specialists, may learn the vocabulary for each search engine/database, the tendency is to use the same search techniques on all systems. This is particularly true for cross-system searching tools that use standards such as Z39.50[14] or OAI-PMH[15] to search individual systems. These tools quicken the information retrieval process as they search many systems concurrently, but the local subtleties and enhancements of the individual underlying systems are negated by the need to group information together semantically using the searching standards. However, there is an acknowledgment in the development of tools such as Google Scholar that the concepts of relevance and quality are important to some topics. Google Scholar limits the harvesting/indexing domain to sites which are considered to be academic and high quality, thus building a quality factor into the search engine.

The cult of personality in this new wired world is being mirrored from the external world. It is easy to adopt new identities in chat rooms or personal e-mail addresses where the names can reflect how one would like to be seen, rather than the formal identity that work brings. As personal and work life continue to mingle and diffuse, so the management of identity and roles within the same identity becomes more important.

In the future, people will expect to be permanently connected to the internet in the same way as mobile telephones have altered attitudes to voice communication. The differences between mobile phones and computers will blur. The changes to information technology have meant that readers' expectations regarding the accessibility of material have changed over the last ten years. This is especially noticeable in access to journal articles, where readers expect to be able to find any article, regardless of how old or obscure, electronically – even from document supply services. Ten years ago, readers would have accepted the need to photocopy articles as part of the academic resource discovery phase, now it is an unacceptable delay in the process. The expectation that electronic resources will always be available and accessible without barriers is raising the bar for library and information services to be able to provide the seamless but 24/7 accessibility required.

Services that provide information and access to information need to prepare for a new generation of users who are technologically aware, fully wired up, responsive to the idea of fulfilling different roles and have high availability expectations, but are perhaps less critical of the resources they find.

These changes highlight the issue of the 'quality' of the information retrieved and at what level this needs to be. Students will be introduced to information resources and an awareness of quality as part of information literacy activities. Library and information services have focused in the past in providing high-quality academic resources, but the division between these and other resources is blurring.

Conclusions

The information environment is undergoing a period of change, from the delivery mechanism of materials to the expectations of the users of information services; institutional repositories are a response to some of these changes.

There is a wide range of stakeholders in the process. These can be loosely grouped in four categories: end users, information providers, information mediators and meta-information users. These all have influence in the changing environment but have different viewpoints. Furthermore, the same people in different roles may have different attitudes. All these stakeholders are important, but authors are the key to successful repositories as they create the content.

The changes in journal production and dissemination have opened up content to those who can afford it. Electronic access has changed the way that end users interact with the literature. It has also highlighted the inequalities of the haves and the have-nots, as it is easier to discover an electronic article, but there is also the issue of access rights. The principle underlying open access is one with which most people would sympathise; how to realise it successfully, however, is more complicated.

It is important to take into consideration the changing perspectives of end users. As the generation who have always had internet access come into the workplace, they will expect the computer systems they use to be as flexible as the wikis, blogs and virtual worlds that they have always used. This could be a challenge for effective institutional repositories.

It is with these background issues in mind that the subject of repositories within this book is set into context.

Notes

1. JISC (2007) 'Mission and vision', available at: *http://www.jisc .ac.uk/aboutus/strategy/strategy0709/strategy_mission_vision .aspx* (accessed 6 June 2007).
2. National Information Standards Organization (2005) 'The OpenURL Framework for Context-Sensitive Services', available at: *http://www.niso.org/standards/standard_detail. cfm?std_id=783* (accessed 6 June 2007).
3. EBSCO (year unknown) 'Five year journal price increase history (2002–2006)', available at: *http://www.ebsco.com/ home/catalog/serialsprices/overview-06.pdf* (accessed 6 June 2007).
4. Budapest Open Access Initiative (2002) 'The Budapest Open Access Initiative', available at: *http://www.soros.org/ openaccess/read.shtml* (accessed 6 June 2007).
5. Bethesda Statement on Open Access Publishing (2003) 'The Bethesda Statement on Open Access Publishing', available at: *http://www.earlham.edu/~peters/fos/bethesda.htm* (accessed 6 June 2007).
6. Berlin Declaration on Open Access to Knowledge in the Sciences and Humanities (2003) 'The Berlin Declaration on Open Access to Knowledge in the Sciences and Humanities', available at: *http://oa.mpg.de/openaccess-berlin/berlinde claration.html* (accessed 6 June 2007).
7. Research Councils UK (2006) 'RCUK position on issue of improved access to research outputs', available at: *http://www .rcuk.ac.uk/research/outputs/access/default.htm* (accessed 6 June 2007).

8. Wellcome Trust (2007) 'Wellcome Trust position statement in support of open and unrestricted access to published research', available at: *http://www.wellcome.ac.uk/doc_WTD002766.html* (accessed 6 June 2007).

9. Universities UK (2005) 'Access to research publications: Universities UK position statement', available at: *http://www.universitiesuk.ac.uk/openaccess/OpenAccessUUKPolicyStatementSept2005.pdf* (accessed 6 June 2007).

10. JISC, RIN, CCLRC and RCUK (2006) 'Opening up access to research outputs: questions and answers, v1.3' available from: *http://www.jisc.ac.uk/media/documents/publications/qanda-doc-final.pdf* (accessed 19 June 2007).

11. Commission of the European Communities (2007) 'Communication on scientific information in the digital age: access, dissemination and preservation (COM(2007) 56 final)', available at: *http://ec.europa.eu/research/science-society/document_library/pdf_06/communication-022007_en.pdf* (accessed 6 June 2007).

12. Australian Government Department of Education, Science and Training (2004) 'Accessibility framework', available at: *http://www.dest.gov.au/sectors/research_sector/policies_issues_reviews/key_issues/accessibility_framework/* (accessed 6 June 2007).

13. Rankin, J. for National Library of New Zealand (2005), 'Institutional repositories for the research sector', feasibility study', available at: *http://wiki.tertiary.govt.nz/~Institutional Repositories/Main/ReportOfFindings* (accessed 6 June 2007).

14. Library of Congress (2006) 'Information Retrieval (Z39.50) Application Service Definition and Protocol Specification', available at: *http://www.loc.gov/z3950/agency/* (accessed 11 April 2007).

15. OAI-PMH (2004) 'The Open Archives Initiative Protocol for Metadata Harvesting', available at: *http://www.openarchives.org/OAI/openarchivesprotocol.html* (accessed 11 April 2007).

3

The organisational view

Introduction

This chapter deals with organisation viewpoints and the strategy and policy decisions that need to be made to ensure a successful institutional repository. Having set in place the policy framework and built the repository, it needs to be filled with the output of the institution. This is heavily dependent on the culture of the organisation and the attitudes taken by senior management. Advocacy, training, user support and quality control all play their part in the success of this venture. The choice of repository software is of course important, but this book is not focusing on this, but rather the generic issues involved with repository management.

The starting point is that organisations, especially academic ones, need to take a strategic view of the information landscape, assess the potential changes and the associated impacts in conjunction with the requirements of their organisation. Any organisation that funds an academic library is likely to buy journals. The changes in publishing paradigm and the rise of open access will, however, affect the service provided and present staffing and budgetary implications. For these reasons alone it is important for the library to be involved in an institutional repository project.

An institutional repository fulfils two requirements for an organisation in the present information landscape:

- a method of disseminating outputs under the aegis of the organisation;
- a central location and focus for the collection of the outputs of the organisation.

These requirements can be broadly generalised as outward facing and inward facing. Dissemination shows the quality of the organisation's work to the world, whereas the second requirement is bound up with management of information and issues such as performance monitoring and evaluation. These two requirements therefore have different stakeholders with different viewpoints.

Returning to the groups of stakeholders identified in the first chapter, the end users will benefit from the dissemination aspects of the repository as long as the repository's logical structure and content metadata enable them to locate the information that they require. Information providers, such as the library service, are likely not only to have viewpoints on the use of the service but also are likely to be the ones maintaining it. Authors are the most complex as regardless of the particular software technology chosen, the most difficult task will be changing cultural attitudes and behaviours to ensure that the repository is filled. Academics, on the whole, have more loyalty to their discipline than the organisation to which they belong and so the discipline's attitude to open access and quality control of publications is likely to dominate their approach to a local repository. As can be seen from the discussion in the previous chapter, funding bodies may also influence the culture, as some bodies have definite opinions as to where the result should be located. This is very discipline-based and may cut across the organisation's viewpoint on what should be held in an institutional repository. The wider information environment and domains will affect the culture and behaviour of both the institution and its staff. For an organisation that covers a wide range of disciplines there may be some tension between regarding the level of quality control and the type of material deposited. As such, disciplines such as medicine, which demand a high level of quality control, may not be so happy to be in the same container as subjects that use a different publishing paradigm with different quality control mechanisms. This is a difficult hurdle to cross, however, the institutional repository should mimic the subjects and materials held in the current library and information service collection, where there is no such tension between subjects.

For subjects with a long-established culture of preprinting in subject-based repositories, such as particle physics with arXiv, thought should be given to how to approach the possibility of depositing slightly different versions of the same article in more than one repository. The preferred version for an institutional repository should be the one closest to the final quality-approved version allowed by the publisher, whereas the preprint version, such as would be taken by arXiv, is acknowledged to be the one submitted to be published.

Stakeholders concerned with performance measuring, such as senior management and funding bodies, need to have their needs assessed from the outset, as their requirements may influence how the internal structure of the repository is set up.

An institutional repository does not need to embrace or challenge the changes in culture that open access may bring, but open access does give opportunities to enhance the full-text collection of publications maintained by most academic environments. Additionally, should the open access movement take off, replacing the journal subscription model as the norm, then the authors belonging to that organisation will need a repository to deposit their papers. While for open access purposes it would be perfectly acceptable for these to be deposited in subject-based repositories, this makes it more difficult for the organisation to be able to report on its outputs and maintan a central collection of institutionally-related material.

An institution may have more than one repository for academic information. For example, it may have different repositories for students' electronic theses and the work of its staff. Much of this chapter discusses aspects of good governance of repositories, and applies to any type of repository.

In an ideal world, the author would complete a full and accurate metadata record and attach the full text at the end of the publisher's embargo period. However, this may not happen in real life. The trick is to ensure that inputting the details into the institutional repository has payoffs in other areas. For example, putting the details into the institutional repository means that the publication list for any personal performance review can be automatically generated. The further the institutional repository is embedded in the business processes of the organisation, the more likely it is to succeed.

Open access and other information developments mean that once a repository is developed, then it is likely to be a long-term investment. While the system used to deliver the content and functionality may have a finite lifetime, the service provided and the underlying requirements that it satisfies are unlikely to become obsolete in the medium term. Ensuring that the repository is on good foundations, through both well-considered policy and stable infrastructure is an important part of good governance and in some ways is more important than the content if other third parties are to build services on top of repositories. To get maximum use, a repository has to be reliable and effective.

By ensuring that the decisions and assumptions made at the start of the project are explicitly documented, then the maintenance and support issues are eased through the life of the service. The policy and implementation frameworks should cover the following three main areas: infrastructure sustainability, content decisions and user engagement. The rest of this chapter looks at these different aspects, from the infrastructure to gaining and maintaining content.

Making the case

One of the most important stakeholder groups to persuade at the start of a potential repository project is the senior management who control strategy, policy and budgets.

A business case for a new development needs to be able to persuade those with the authority to approve it that it is a worthwhile if not vital project. To be able to do this, many different aspects as of the project and its context need to be identified and explored. The style and relative importance of the different aspects will alter depending on the audience for the business case, and it is important to understand what will motivate the intended audience to react in a positive manner.

The espida project (*http://www.gla.ac.uk/espida/*), funded by the Joint Information Steering Committee (JISC) has produced a model and handbook[1] for developing project proposals or business cases which can be successfully applied to repository proposals.

The model aims to identify the motivating factors for the decision makers so that the project proposers can write the case in a way that the decision makers can more easily see the benefits. One of the problems for writing a successful case is that information is an intangible asset and difficult to quantify in money terms.

It starts with an understanding of the strategic vision and the context in which the decisions will be made. These are then viewed from four standpoints:

- *customer and external stakeholders*: the contribution made by the project to satisfying their needs and the subsequent enhancement of reputation;

- *innovation and development*: the contribution to the intellectual output of the organisation and an innovative working environment;

- *internal business process*: contribution to the way the organisation works or could work better;

- *financial*: contribution to the bottom line through savings or income generation.

Within each of these areas, there will be specific elements or outcome indicators. Each of these will have an impact, whether positive or negative, on likelihood and timescales. Using these then a case can be built. The specific elements are closely linked to the organisation and the particular set of stakeholders and so cannot be generalised; however, the different standpoints are likely to apply to all organisations.

So, for example, if the funding for the repository project is coming from more than one source, using this model might show how best to communicate the case to the different parties.

Infrastructure and sustainability

Deciding to implement an institutional repository is a long-term commitment and thus consideration of the technical infrastructure and financial issues involved in running a high-visibility and possibly high-impact service is essential.

In this context, infrastructure is taken to mean the hardware and software chosen to run the repository together with the associated support functions to enable the system to run effectively.

The first decision to make is regarding the appropriate software for the organisation's needs and the hardware to support this.

Choosing repository software

As with any new system, the starting point is a requirements gathering exercise with as many of the key stakeholders as possible. This should enable the project team to draw up a specification of what is required. In this type of exercise it is always a good idea to attempt to set priorities for the requirements, i.e. deciding between *mandatory* ones, without which the system will not be satisfactory, and *optional* ones, which would enhance the functionality of the system but would not stop the process. With a clear understanding of what is required, and hopefully some sense of any specialist organisational requirements that might not form part of a standard service, the project team can look at the available systems to decide on what best meets the needs of the organisation.

Factors that might influence this decision include whether there is any organisational policy on whether this type of system is supported internally or outsourced to a third party. There is also the consideration of the staff expertise available – will they have the skills and the time to be able to install and modify or set up the chosen system as required? Although the offerings in the repository field are open source, several companies do offer supported services for these products, thus giving the option to choose whether to support the repository internally or externally. As the present focus is on the content and cultural issues of repositories, however, any discussion of the individual software products on offer is beyond the remit of this book.

The requirement exercise will be influential in setting the remit of the system and subsequently generating an explicit statement of purpose. This statement makes clear what the service does, who are the main stakeholders and who is responsible for it and the constituent parts. This ensures clear lines of responsibility and a fixed point to refer to if there are any questions in the future.

Infrastructure requirements

Regardless of the decisions made on the software to be used and the associated support, there will be both set-up and ongoing costs. Taking the in-house service provision, the following areas need to be considered:

- *Hardware*: The purchase cost of the equipment on which the service runs, if it is to be a dedicated service, in addition to a rolling replacement/upgrade schedule to ensure that the hardware remains in a suitable condition for providing the service. Any support costs in maintaining computer equipment on site should also be identified. These costs should include any that result from running equipment, such as backups and security patching the operating system.

- *Software*: Although there may not be any direct costs for the software, there may be costs involved in belonging to user groups or other support communities.

- *Staffing*: There will be some staff costs involved with the technical running of the service, such as installation of software upgrades and ensuring that the security patches for the hardware are up to date.

Policy decisions on infrastructure

Purchasing decisions are as important as technical considerations regarding the implementation and maintenance of software. Depending on how the infrastructure is supported, these issues may be subject to other services' policies. All decisions should be documented for reference.

Software upgrades

Current software is under development to ensure that it stays in step with changing requirements. This development is usually staged by the software author providing software releases with discrete additional functionality and associated documentation. There may also be bug fix releases or patches which can be applied to fix particular problems discovered after the main release. This brings a host of decisions about upgrading the software:

- *Who will perform them?* This may be set by the support mechanisms that have been put in place. It is important to be clear about who will do the upgrades and whether they have the right skills.

- *What external factors may affect the timing of upgrades?* This could reflect the needs of the organisation or the support team.

- *What position does the project take on when to upgrade?* Being one of the first to upgrade means that the new features are available sooner, but also brings the risk of finding problems which were not discovered during the beta-testing. However, always being one of the last to upgrade implies not benefiting from new features, and there may be pressure from software suppliers/supporters to upgrade at a time which may not be as convenient for the organisation.

- *Is a test server necessary?* This gives an opportunity to test the new version before it goes out into the public domain. If the system is complex or very high profile then the additional expense that a test server provides is negated by the benefits it brings.

- *What acceptance tests will there be and who will perform them?* After any upgrade it is important to ensure that the system is behaving as expected; acceptance testing with prearranged criteria is an effective method. As this needs to be done as soon as possible after the upgrade, then it is important to ensure that there are testers available and that they are able to perform the tests adequately.

Customisation

Intertwined with software upgrades are the decisions made on local customisation of the software. In this context, this entails more than just setting up the policies and settings of the software but actually modifying the functionality. One of the benefits of open source software is than it is possible to modify the underlying structure to one's needs and that such developments can be shared within the community. The points to be considered here are:

- *What is the policy on customising the software and adding local tweaks?* This is of course dependent on having the necessary skills available locally, although the project team may decide that this is not appropriate even if the skills are available.

- *Will these customisations need redoing after upgrades or could they be adopted by the developers to become part of the final version?* When choosing to tweak the software it is important to keep a record of what has been done and be prepared to reinstate in the latest version if the tweak is not adopted by the developers.

Standards compliance

As the repository field is a new and developing one, some parts of the system have more agreed standards than others. Some standards, such as OAI-PMH, are part of the software and are well developed. The standards on metadata are still under development. All systems are able to provide Dublin Core output, but this is not descriptive enough to be able to ensure complete interoperability and transfer of data between different systems. Thus, although much of this area is fixed, there should be policy regarding what metadata standards have been chosen and complied with.

Preservation or curation approaches

The general approach to this may have influenced the infrastructure choices made and this area overlaps with the content discussed in subsequent chapters. However, the preservation approach over the long term will have an effect on the financial sustainability of the service. The issues to consider are:

- *What data migration and preservation strategies will be adopted and does this apply to the whole collection or specialised subsets?*

- *At what stage are preservation actions going to take place?* As an institutional repository holds the full text of scholarly works, then the issues around accessibility of the format of the electronic file become important. There are two obvious options to dealing with file preservation: the first is for the system to convert any deposited file to a known format and then preserve this; the second is to take any file format but have a process to identify file formats that are becoming obsolete and then migrate those to a newer format. Both these choices have pros and cons and are discussed in more detail in Chapter 5.

- *Is the preservation going to be done in-house?* An alternative to doing in-house preservation is the possibility of outsourcing to a third party. These services are still under development but it is very likely that they will be established before long.

Staff learning and development

A system is only as good as the support staff and so their learning and development needs should be taken into consideration. As such, the mechanisms and costs for ensuring that staff are up to date with developments is an important area.

Service delivery

Once the infrastructure and policy decisions are in place and documented then there should be structures in place to ensure the smooth running of the service. An important part of this is a business continuity plan. This identifies the risks associated with the service, identifies mitigation procedures and outlines strategies for service continuation in a disaster recovery plan. If possible, the recovery plan should be tested before any real disaster happens to ensure that it is accurate. These plans and procedures should be checked every 6–12 months for accuracy. Examples of areas to consider include:

- *Damage to the IT infrastructure providing the service*: This is a low-risk but high-impact possibility. This is mitigated by ensuring that the equipment is appropriate for the tasks, that procedures are in place for patching the operating systems to ensure no security loopholes, that appropriate backup strategy is identified and in place, and that there is a disaster recovery plan.

- *Staffing problems, such as succession planning, skills gaps etc.*: Ensure that the skills are known, and wherever possible there is multiskilling and that the documentation is adequate.

- *Funding*: This depends on local circumstances, but it should always be a risk and should be mitigated as appropriate.

- *Not achieving strategic goals*: If the project is not a success, what will the impact be, and what steps are in place to ensure that it is a success?

- *Physical damage to the building*: This covers things like aeroplanes landing onsite; the impacts should be covered by the disaster recovery plan.

Financial sustainability

While it is understandable that new pilot projects might be funded through shifting priorities or special projects, once the institutional repository is embedded into the business process of the organisation, more long-term funding mechanisms should be explored to ensure that the service is on an even keel. As the trend for IT costs is decreasing year on year, it is likely that most of the expenditure in the long term will be related to staff rather than capital outlay on equipment.

Content

This is the most important area as an empty repository, even one with very clear policies, is of no use without any content. However, there are many decisions to be made about the content to ensure that it is fit for purpose and satisfies as many stakeholder groups as possible.

- *What material types is it designed to hold?* It is important to be clear about the different types of content that the repository is intended to collect. There will be different description requirements, preservation issues and potentially workflow associated with different types of material deposited. Are there special issues with any of them? Metadata requirements should be considered for each of the material types likely to be deposited and the mandatory subset of these identified so that everyone understands what constitutes a minimal record. Checks can then be done to see if this satisfies the minimum requirements of the system.

- *Who is entitled to deposit content?* Closely aligned to the purpose of the repository and the decisions on material types is the expectation of who is entitled to deposit content within the repository.

- *Who do you expect to be the main content builder?* Are the authors likely to self-deposit or will they get someone else to do it for them? Will professional cataloguers be involved in the process? The help, training and guidance through the input workflow depends on the level of knowledge of bibliographic references and what information is associated with them. The level of interest and ability of the inputers also influences the quality of the metadata.

- *How will the repository be structured?* The internal structure of the repository will influence the access points to the content and probably the statistical analysis available, so it is an important issue to get right. How easy will it be for the inputer to be able to locate the data for the structure? For example, if the intention is to mirror the organisational structure, will this be obvious from the information the depositor will be looking at? Thought should also be given for future-proofing this structure, for example, what will be done if a department alters?

- *Will there be data validation and checking?* The institutional repository is a visible system and most of the input is likely to be done by people with minimal training. What processes will be put in place to ensure consistency and accuracy of information? Consideration should be made of the types of checks that should be done, their frequency and who is likely to be performing them.

- *What is the position on retrospective information?* There are two approaches to content in institutional repositories: one starts with a blank canvas when the repository goes live and concentrates on getting new content, usually with the full text; the second is to populate the repository with information from other systems which are more likely to be metadata records only. The benefits of starting from fresh is that all the metadata and content comply to the standards of this particular system and are likely to be consistent, however, it may be difficult to get content as there is no critical mass. On the other hand, the benefit of adding retrospective content is that it is more likely to have critical mass and, for authors, more of their publication history will be available in one place. However, the metadata is less likely to be as consistent and it is more likely that full-text content will not be not available. This is a choice for the project team influenced by organisational requirements.

- *Access to content*: Once there is full-text content within the system, there needs to be a policy framework to define the rights and responsibilities of both the depositing author and the repository. The author needs to give the repository the right to disseminate the work and the rights to be able to copy it for preservation and migration reasons. There also needs to be policies in place about depositing items with embargo periods or restricted viewing public and associated procedures.

- *Removal policy*: As well as having clear policy on what is added to the repository and what is preserved for the long term, there should also be some policy about withdrawing content. The repository manager is responsible for ensuring access is not provided to content that is illegal or defamatory, as well as establishing a process for removing such material once it has been brought to their attention. The withdrawal policy needs to consider how complete the withdrawal process needs to be. Should all mention of the item be removed or is it acceptable to retain the metadata record?

One of the major issues around content is whether deposit in the repository is going to be voluntary or mandatory. If it is voluntary then there will be a keen set of early adopters who will enter information, but it will not cover the whole of the organisation's output. To make it mandatory requires support from senior management.

One approach to this problem is the patchwork mandate.[2] This suggests starting at the departmental management level and getting one department at a time to mandate staff to deposit. It is suggested that this is likely to be more successful with staff as they have stronger allegiance to their department and, over time, the entire organisation may mandate. This ties in with common themes to user engagement and advocacy discussed in the next section.

User engagement and advocacy

Once the collection remit and general policy decisions have been made, the focus needs to shift to engaging the user community and the advocacy needed to achieve this. As outlined elsewhere, there are many stakeholders in the institutional repository but the key ones are the authors who produce the content that should be deposited in the repository. Here there are two parts to a successful partnership between depositor and repository: a clear understanding of the purpose and remit of the repository and ensuring that the deposit process is as straightforward and time-efficient as possible. Interacting with authors is where the culture of the organisation and subject domain comes into play as, on the surface, the authors are those with the least clear immediate personal benefits in the process. Assuming that the author is prepared to self-deposit, they have the added task of making the deposit using the provided workflow mechanism, but having done so, the benefits are intangible unless the repository is embedded in organisational processes such as personal reviews. Of course, depositing their work in a publicly accessible repository raises their profile and makes their work more accessible, but this is not linked to the actual point in time when the work is done to deposit the item. The benefits to a depositor need to be promoted as the rate of citations and visibility will increase and they can reuse this information themselves in personal reviews and other areas where a publication list is needed.

Continuing with the theme of authors, there are some readily identifiable external influences on the researcher on their attitude to using an institutional repository:

- *Department policy*: It has been shown that department policy has a great influence over researchers' behaviour. This level of the organisation is closer to the researcher and in turn they are likely to have more say in it. In other words, the carrots and sticks are closer to hand!

- *Funder policy*: The funder of the research holds both power and influence depending on their position and enforcement of the position. If future funds depend on complying with present policy then that is a keen driver of deposition.

- *Domain attitudes*: Many studies have shown that the attitude of the subject area will greatly influence researcher – unless of course they are a 'trail blazer'.

- *Organisation policy*: This is similar to the departmental policy but can seem more remote and passed down as 'tablets of stone'.

The repository manager should be aware that the wider organisational stakeholders, such as department heads, need to be influenced as much as individual authors.

Getting content: advocacy themes and aims

To be successful with all the users and stakeholders involved in institutional repository building the advocacy campaign should be planned in an organised fashion. The general points to start the planning process with might include:

- *Which group of stakeholders to start with?* Will it be most effective to start with a certain set of stakeholders and if so who are they? There are many ways of subdividing organisational stakeholders, but in this case the two obvious ones are by seniority and by organisational structure. Depending on the process to start the repository project, there may already be buy-in from senior management, which is crucial to ensure that the repository is sustainable over the long term; however, this set of people may not be key in influencing authors to deposit content.

- *Understand the discipline differences*: As discipline is a key influencer on behaviour it is therefore important to understand the differences in publishing patterns and general attitudes to open access. This will help the campaign as it will give some idea of what the community in that subject area can be expected to know about the topic in general. If the organisation has subject liaison librarians, these can be employed to interact on the subject.

- *Identify key organisational committees*: Hand in hand with understanding the stakeholder groups and discipline differences is knowing the key internal committees who are likely to discuss these topics, to ensure the project team is invited to any influential discussions.

- *Identify early adopters of open access principles*: These early adopters might be a local enthusiast or an entire subject domain. For example, those particle physicists who are involved with the Large Hadron Collider at CERN are having a very vibrant debate about open access publishing as of spring 2007. This has been brought on by scientists within the community rather than library services. These keen researchers can bring more gravitas to the advocacy work as they are respected by their peers.

- *Identify areas with complicated requirements*: Having done the analysis of the disciplines supported by the organisation, identify any of those whose requirements are likely to be complicated and difficult to achieve, and tackle these after more straightforward areas. It is easier to persuade difficult areas to use a system which is successfully in use by the majority of the organisation than to get people to use a system whose early adopters have had nothing but problems.

- *Be responsive to criticism*: If during these sessions the same issues are raised again and again, then try to address them by changing the way the repository is implemented. It is far easier to modify software than to modify user behaviour.

- *Publicity*: Consider what type of publicity will be the most effective. This could range from one-to-one sessions, group sessions or articles in the local news sheet. Ensure that the content is applicable for the medium chosen.

- *Branding*: Consider the brand and the name of the service before the publicity starts as these are crucial in successful publicity and marketing.

Content of advocacy sessions

While the audience and occasion will define the type of advocacy used to get the message across, the key messages to get across will include:

- *Information landscape and open access*: Although the circumstances that started the repository may not be directly related to open access, it is a major influence in the development and direction of institutional repositories. It is also useful to be able to show that repositories and access to information is not just limited to the needs of the local institution but is part of a wider arena.

- *What is an institutional repository and why should anyone have one?* This leads on from the wider point and explains the concepts and the benefits of change to the relevant stakeholder.

- *The local policy on content*: This is an opportunity to explain what is expected to be deposited, suitable formats and some explanation on the curation policy.

- *Local policy on who inputs the content, and any approval/checking mechanisms*: This is an opportunity to discuss who is likely to deposit the content, and what type of training and documentation they might require. The approval and data checking procedures also fall into this area.

- *Removal policy*: As discussed earlier in this chapter, it is important to be clear about how items are removed and what content is unacceptable.

- *Demonstration of the system*: In many advocacy situations, finishing with a well-prepared demonstration showing the important features is always a good endpoint. If the system is still under development and can be unreliable, then the same effect can be achieved using a slideshow and screenshots. It is important to remember that this may be the group's first exposure to the system, and it will negatively affect their impression of it if the demonstration doesn't go smoothly.

Training and documentation

As part of the advocacy process, there is likely to be some content concerned with training and documentation. There are three types of repository user who might require documentation and training: the end users of the information who need to know how to locate information, the author or author's intermediary who inputs the metadata and the associated digital object, and system administrators. As the end users may also be authors, in most cases it is probably most effective to combine both aspects of using the system in the same session.

There are many ways of conducting user training and, to a certain extent, the most successful method will be depend on the culture of the organisation and the type of people being trained. One important factor when thinking about the training process is to consider the needs of existing staff who need to understand the new system and new staff who will need to understand both the system and the organisation. Taking new staff first, it would be most effective to include the institutional repository and the institutional policies about it as part of induction training.

End users and authors

The end users represent a wide range of people within the organisation and may include library staff using the repository to answer enquiries, or authors using the repository at the endpoint of a research project/piece of work. It may be viewed as an administrative task rather than a dissemination route.

Training might include one or more of the following methods:

- department briefing and/or sessions, where domain-specific issues can be addressed;
- formal training events;
- drop-in sessions at set times;
- one-to-one sessions – useful for those people who are likely to input a lot or for important stakeholders who need to have a positive learning experience.

Although one might hope that the system is self-explanatory, the use of attractive documentation can add to the advocacy sessions. Useful types of written material might include:

- *quick start*: short but attractive leaflets with enough information to make a start;
- *user manuals*: more in-depth works with information on more unusual material types and more guidance on local rules;
- *help and on-screen guidance*: aiding the user during the input process, especially with onscreen guidance can be the most effective method of ensuring that users follow best practice and local rules;
- *news articles*: in in-house magazines and other publicity material.

System administrators

As well as any system documentation provided with the chosen software, there needs to be local documentation about the set-up and policy decisions made as part of the implementation project.

Maintaining content

As institutional repositories grow in number and importance in the information landscape, so the quality of repository content will be used as an indicator of the quality of the repository as a resource. As such, validation and verification of the data are an important factor.

There are two levels to this task: the metadata about a particular scholarly work and the organisational and contextual information about that work. To be able to do either effectively the previously discussed content policy must have been created, and training and documentation must be available to ensure that the users are aware of the standards required.

Considering the metadata about a particular work then ensuring appropriate quality is not a trivial task given the potential data flow into the system. The starting point for this is to decide what, if any, quality measures are going to be implemented and then the most appropriate process for achieving this can be chosen. Table 3.1 outlines some of the possible metadata problems that might occur when significant numbers of authors are inputting their works into an institutional repository.

The organisational context refers to areas such as linking the work to a particular project, department or the organisational context of the author. Organisations change to meet the needs of their stakeholders, and this is often

Table 3.1 Metadata issues and mitigation method

Issue	Description	Mitigation methods
Duplicates	Where separate authors have put the same record in again without checking if it is already there	Automatic check in input process Exception report looking for identical titles Documentation for input
Incorrect journal titles	Where the journal title can't be identified uniquely from the input, especially if abbreviations have been used.	Validated list to choose from Exception reporting looking for similar journal titles
Misspelt words	Typing errors etc.	These are very difficult to spot or find automatically
Missing fields	All the important fields are likely to be mandatory but there may be some which are optional and are more useful if completed.	Leave as is Run exception reports to find empty fields
Incorrect references to the formally published work	The reference to the published work is incorrectly input	This would be difficult to check by eye as it requires a lot of knowledge about the item in question If DOIs are looked-up automatically then exception reports from this process could identify problem records
Different styles in text	Authors inputting entire entry in capitals or other input quirks	Automatic conversion by the system to preferred format Leave as is Documentation for input

reflected in the internal structure. If the repository reflects this in the way it is structured or information is retrieved then the policy to this issue must be addressed.

There can be tensions in trying to attribute the works to the right organisational structure. For repository managers it is important that the correct structure is shown, however, they may wish to collate several structural changes into one historical look for other stakeholders. For example:

Researcher A has worked in Institution W for 10 years, during this time he has remained in the same research area, however the department has altered from Technology to Instrumentation and then to Engineering and Instrumentation. The last change was a merger with the Engineering department. This could be represented as:

Department of Engineering *1987 – 2004*
Department of Engineering and Instrumentation *2004 – date*
Department of Instrumentation *2000 – 2004*
Department of Technology *1998 – 2000*

To be able to get a long-term view of the work of this subject domain, there needs to be some understanding of how these instances relate to each other.

Once the decisions of the type and detail of quality control and validation have been made, the most appropriate processes should be identified. The repository should be set up to ensure that all the required information is entered and wherever it is important to ensure data consistency, such as with organisational structure, that this is either automatically identified from the user or chosen from fixed sets of options. Having ensured that the data is as accurate as possible, there are two obvious points where there could be some additional checking:

- During the input process through an approval checking stage:
  - *advantages*: ensures that the quality standards are checked and applied before the information is available

to all, making it easier to identify spelling errors if all entries are checked;

- *disadvantages*: may introduce time delays, especially if there are large input flows; also entails staff time spent checking for potential errors when there may be none to find.

■ After the input process through exception checking reports:

- *advantages*: staff time used to correct records that have been identified as not meeting quality standards;

- *disadvantages*: records not meeting the standards have been publicly available; basic spelling mistakes may not be located as these can be hard to identify automatically.

Although any sort of validation and verification will be staff-intensive, it is an area best done by those professionally trained to understand the importance of metadata accuracy and is an area where the library and information services can add value to the service provided. If it is compared with the effort undertaken to manage the journals collections or the catalogue to the library's holdings then it can be put into perspective.

Retrospective content

It is important to define the starting point for the repository's collection. In many cases, the repository will replace systems which have collected information on publications, possibly without access to the full text of the work. It is worthwhile considering whether to import these records into the repository. While these records may only contain the bibliographic record, they will add critical mass to the repository, making it seem more useful and relevant from the start. One of the major factors for making this decision is the attitude taken to the content from the stakeholders: is this repository's aim to be an open access repository with all entries linked to the publicly accessible full text wherever possible, or is the primary function to record the outputs of the organisation? This decision must be made in accordance with the culture and stakeholders' requirements.

If the library is registered with CrossRef then one can programmatically look up the DOIs and add these to the records. While this is not meeting the open access full-text ideal, at least it is offering full text for those readers who subscribe to the publication.

Roles and responsibilities

This chapter has discussed some of the issues involved in setting up and running an institutional repository. Key to the success of this is the staff who support the repository. There are a number of roles and responsibilities that can be identified and need to be fulfilled, by one or many different people. As this is a developing field, roles and responsibilities are not completely defined, but drawing on my own experience I feel that there is the need for expertise at different organisational levels, with different foci to enable the repository to be successful. These are summarised below:

- *Repository management*: responsible for decision making, sustainability issues, advocacy with senior stakeholders and policy making. This role is to ensure that the repository is effective within the organisation, is sufficiently resourced and additionally may have a wider role to liaise with the external repository community to adopt standards and to share best practice.

- *Repository administration*: responsible for ensuring the uptake on the ground, for data quality, user support, guidance and training. This role is closer to the authors and those who actually input data and so can monitor the uptake and quality and feed this back to be able to enhance the repository in the future.

■ *Systems support*: responsible for providing technical support to ensure that the infrastructure is reliable and effective.

Areas such as general advocacy and training are not necessarily fixed to a particular role as these skills are usually associated with the person in the post rather than a role at a particular level in the organisation.

Conclusions

Once the organisation has decided to implement a repository, the hardware and software infrastructure needs to be put in place and any decisions documented. For successful content generation, careful thought must be given to which community members should be approached first and what aspects of a repository will motivate them to get involved. Once content has started to be input, there are new issues around maintaining it, including validation and verification. This chapter has been full of questions to be considered, but has not offered any definite answers. This is because every organisation is different and the answers need to satisfy local requirements.

Notes

1. Glasgow DSpace Service (2007) 'espida handbook. Expressing project costs and benefits in a systematic way for investment in information and IT', available at: *http://hdl.handle.net/1905/691* (accessed 11 April 2007).
2. Sale, A. (2007) 'The patchwork mandate', *D-Lib Magazine* 13 (1/2), available at: *http://www.dlib.org/ dlib/january07/sale/ 01sale.html* (accessed 11 April 2007).

4

Content decisions

Introduction

This chapter discusses what the content of an institutional repository might be, what the cultural and legal issues involved are, and touches on the complicated issue of versions and being able to identify which version has been located.

In the preceding chapters the environmental and organisational framework has been described, looking at content from various high-level aspects. The present chapter considers the content and how it might be described and located. As a starting point, there is a discussion about how a conceptual model for describing bibliographic records might inform the repository and which metadata standards are used in this area.

The metadata standards and schema to be used define and constrain the eventual use of the repository. Using lightweight standards ensures that the creation of the metadata used to retrieve information will be easy to achieve, although the longer-term potential for reuse may decline as the descriptions may be not rich enough. On the other hand, using rich and expansive standards may mean that there are learning curve problems with completing the information, which may introduce inconsistencies. As repositories are designed so that those once considered end users can input metadata, a straightforward method of ensuring consistency of data quality within the repository is important. Library catalogues and other information resources have been produced by people who are trained to use precise rules and conventions, who understand the importance of accuracy for retrieval and that the information in such resources is on public display. This is not true when asking authors or local departmental administrators to input metadata. It is likely to be considered to be an administrative task which should take the minimum effort.

The stakeholders identified in Chapter 2 have different needs for the metadata used to describe and locate the content. End users need enough information about the content from the resource discovery service to ascertain whether it will be of use to them. Identifying the type of material found is an important part of this process. Authors who intend to deposit the material themselves need to understand the process and know how much metadata is required. The organisation and the project team need to ensure that there is sufficient information for discovery as well as sufficient information for managing and reporting on the collection. By using metadata standards and protocols, third-party service providers can use the information within the system for other purposes, widening the dissemination remit.

Understanding the context and culture will inform the decisions about the metadata to be collected, such as what needs to be made mandatory and what can remain optional, while ensuring that the requirements of the repository from other stakeholders are met.

Conceptual models of information

One of the conceptual models in this area has been developed by the International Federation of Library

Associations (IFLA) and is called Functional Requirements for Bibliographic Records (FRBR).[1]

The model identifies four entities needed to describe a bibliographic work together with an entity relating to agents and the actions they perform on the bibliographic record. The four entities relate different facets of information about a work, from the abstract idea to a particular physical instance. In this hierarchy some information is common to all levels and some is introduced to deal with the particular level. Figure 4.1 shows the bibliographic entities.

The figure breaks the information required into four levels where *Work* represents a particular conceptual idea. This does not have any physical embodiment on its own – this is done by describing expressions of the work. An example of this might be Handel's 'Messiah': this has been realised in many different scores and recordings, but these all relate to the same intellectual content. If there are several expressions of the abstract idea with different intellectual content by different people (agents), then each of these becomes a new work. A good example of this is the abstract concept of 'Romeo and Juliet'. This has been realised in many forms, including a play by Shakespeare and music by Prokofiev, which has been used in a ballet with choreography. These different realisations are different works. However, the abstract concept is used to link together different versions of the same work.

Figure 4.1   **FRBR entities**

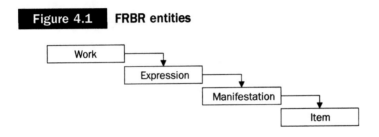

Expression is a particular version or representation of the idea with some distinct intellectual content. If describing an existing item there will always be at least one expression. Due to different editions of the same item, or the same concept rendered in different ways, there may well be more. Examples of this are the English text and a French translation, or a journal article and conference presentation covering the same material, or different performances of an artist's work. It is up to the discretion of the cataloguer when the change is sufficient for the item to be described as a new work.

Manifestation is a physical representation of the expression and the first point where consideration of the actual format is made; there is always at least one. The expression could be realised, for example, by a print run, a piece of art or a digital object. A digital object with the same intellectual content but in a different format is a different manifestation of the same expression. Other examples of this are a recording of the same performance, but one on DVD and one on video.

Item describes a particular representation of the manifestation. There is always one, but this need not be a single entity as there may be many physical items for some manifestations. Good examples of this are paper encyclopaedias or a television series on multiple DVDs. This item may have notes associated with it that only pertain to that particular copy; these might relate to location or physical appearance.

This layered approach to describing things from the abstract idea to one particular physical item, mirrors the approach taken in many information resources. Many resources have more than one copy of something and therefore wish to group them together. This model allows for that but also gives the benefit of linking together works that are similar but not the same.

Figure 4.2   **Example of FRBR**

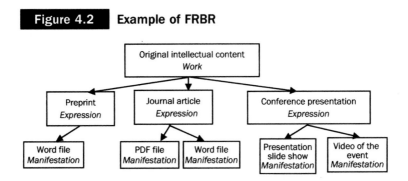

Although FRBR was written with a library catalogue and physical items at the forefront; the distinctions made are relevant in an electronic world. Scholarly work can be a complex structure of interrelated works. These relationships can be made explicit by using the FRBR conceptual model. Multiple expressions of a work may be available through preprinting or deposition in an open access repository and FRBR gives one way of being able to identify the intellectual or physical differences between the items retrieved. The main disadvantage to this model is being able to apply consistency in deciding when there are enough differences to warrant designating the work as new.

Figure 4.2 illustrates this with the example of an author who does some research and produces a conclusion, which is presented at conference and then written up for a journal article. For each of the entries for the particular material types, there should ideally be full-text content. This content corresponds with particular instances of the FRBR manifestations as represented by the material types.

Metadata standards

There are many metadata standards available but the baseline for interoperability in this field is Dublin Core.[2]

This standard has its roots in web-based discovery and was developed to describe this type of material in a uniform manner rather than library-specific material. While Dublin Core has strengths and is widely adopted, some of the original terms are ambiguous and need further clarification. Dublin Core is maintained by the Dublin Core Metadata Initiative (*http://dublincore.org/*). As Dublin Core is the lingua franca of the web world, it is important to be able to generate this, regardless of what internal standards are used to describe the objects.

The original set is as follows:

- *contributor*: an entity responsible for making contributions to the content of the resource, typically a person or an organisation;
- *coverage*: extent or scope on the content of the resource;
- *creator*: an entity primarily responsible for making the content of a resource, typically a person or an organisation;
- *date*: associated with the lifecycle of the resource, typically the creation date;
- *description*: an account of the resource;
- *format*: the physical or digital manifestation of the resource;
- *identifier*: unambiguous reference to the resource in a given context;
- *language*: language of the intellectual content of the resource;
- *publisher*: entity responsible for making the resource available;
- *relation*: a reference to a related resource;
- *rights management*: information about rights held in and over the resource;

- *source*: reference to a resource from which the present resource is derived;
- *subject*: topic of the content of the resource;
- *title*: a name given to the resource;
- *type*: nature or genre of the content of the resource.

The main issue with using simple Dublin Core to describe content within a bibliographic context is that these fields do not have enough expressiveness to describe the content precisely.

Taking a couple of the fields as examples: the *contributor* field does not describe what type of contributor has been made the contribution: is it an author or an editor or another role? The *date* field is another one where it is not precise enough. What date is being definitely referred to? Is it the creation date or some other one?

To resolve these and other issues there are now extensions to cover better temporal understanding, collection management, better rights management and relationships to other material.

An initiative to improve this for the open access repository environment is the development of an application profile for scholarly works.[3] The application profile defines the use of the Dublin Core fields more precisely and sets rules for the content. This particular profile uses the concepts from FRBR to define Dublin Core terms with clear definitions for use by institutional repositories. If a repository adopted this, data exports could include a Dublin Core scholarly works application profile for services that are able to understand and use this more detailed information as well as providing straightforward Dublin Core.

It breaks the metadata required for a scholarly work into five sections:

- *the scholarly work*: title, creator, subject, funding information and abstract;

- *an expression of the scholarly work*: title, description, status, language, versioning information, dates, citation, references and identifier;

- *the manifestation*: format, publisher, where available;

- *the copy*: access right, date available, licence information;

- *the agent*: name, workplace homepage, mailbox and identifier.

The enhanced expressiveness and awareness of the context can be shown by taking the creator as an example. Using this application profile, the creator is further defined from the Dublin Core standpoint of 'an entity primarily responsible for making the content of the resource' to be *an author of the e-print* and the notes specify that the expected input is a name or a uniform resource identifier (URI) link to a person. By the instructions and definitions, the role of the creator is explicitly stated to be the author of the intellectual work.

While many of the fields have clearer instructions regarding the content, the most important additions specific to the institutional repository are information on the peer-review status of the item and additional information on the funding, including the grant and supervisor if appropriate.

It is unlikely that strict Dublin Core or even the scholarly works profile will capture all the information required for full functionality of a repository. Some of this additional information may be specific to the organisation, while others may be of a standard bibliographic format, and still others may be able to preserve the information in the longer term. The latter is dealt with in Chapter 5.

As yet there is no overall detailed standard in use for all repositories as there is in library catalogues with MARC.[4]

If the MARC style approach and level of detail is important then the Metadata Object Description Schema (MODS),[5] which has been developed by the Library of Congress and the MARC Standards Office, might be the way to go. With the trend in information resource description to use XML[6] as the standard for web-based resources, MARC21 has been adapted to the XML standard as MARCXML. It was acknowledged that MARCXML and MARC21 may be too rich for some purposes and so MODS was developed. As part of the development process it supports or extends METS (described in Chapter 5) and harvesting protocols. As it is based on a widely used library standard, the metadata created using MODS is compatible with existing information resources.

The high-level elements are:

- Element (information)
- titleInfo (information about the title, including if it has an alternative etc.)
- name (name, including type, role and affiliation)
- typeOfResource (from a set of values describing possible works)
- genre (type of material)
- originInfo (place, publisher, date (created, captured, valid, modified, copyright and other), edition and frequency)
- language (of the work)
- physicalDescription (form, digital origin and preservation details)
- abstract
- tableOfContents
- targetAudience

- note
- subject (type of subject term, such as topic, temporal, geographic etc)
- classification (including the scheme used)
- relatedItem (type of relation and the link)
- identifier
- location (physical location and/or URL)
- accessCondition
- part (ordering information)
- extension
- recordInfo (information on record and coding scheme used)

The ability to go into detail at a greater granularity shows the MARC origins of MODS and gives it expressiveness that Dublin Core is unable to match. Depending on the needs of the repository, and who is intended to complete the metadata, this may give too great a level of detail. However, it is easier to reduce expressive metadata than to be able to produce information that was not originally collected. MODS shows its origins from the specialised world of librarianship and cataloguing.

Although one can expose all types of metadata within the OAI-PMH interface,[8] the most common standard is Dublin Core and this should be provided for others so that they can easily use your data.

Whatever metadata schema is chosen to suit the needs of the repository and the organisation, as long as it is documented and the data within it is consistent, then it will always be possible to transfer it to another system, as a 'cross-walk' can be generated to map fields from one system to another.

Types of material and their differences

A research institution may produce many difference types of research output, from data collected from an experiment, through software to written publications and one-off performances in the arts. In some disciplines, access to the research record is a straightforward and well understood process, in others it is more complicated and related to the output itself. This section outlines some of the more common types of material that might be deposited in a repository, any particular issues to note as a result and alternative locations and methods of finding the material. Certain types of output which are more difficult to generalise or which are less understood have been excluded, these include software and archival versions of websites.

A more interesting issue is data. Data is not a homogeneous collection always requiring similar metadata. It is a very complex domain and sometimes even a project-specific area. It underpins the scholarly communication cycle in many disciplines but is not always formally recognised in the same way as publication has been. The data produced can be both small and large-scale. It may be the result of a small project or experiment or part of a large-scale and long-term project. These require different preservation and access techniques. Many of the funders of projects that generate data require the project investigator to make a plan for the data before any is collected and they may also require that it is deposited in a national or international data centre so that it can be reused by the community. In my personal opinion, specialist data is best in a specialist repository maintained by domain experts.

Although it is clear how an institutional repository benefits the organisation, using a subject-based repository may have some appeal to those working in a particular subject. In some areas, such as biological sciences with PubMedCentral and PubMedUK, the subject-based repository is the first port of call. In these cases, the repository manager needs to consider whether it would be more effective to concentrate on harvesting mechanisms from these subject repositories, or linking to the full text held there.

In addition to specialised information, the material under consideration will have metadata elements in common with other types of material. For example, when considering the information required for the material types described here, one might expect them all to have a title and an author; in contrast only conference-related material would have information to identify the conference, such as name, dates, organisers and location. It is important to be aware of the similarities and differences in the requirements for descriptive metadata. Material types are presented in alphabetical order below.

Books and book chapters

As books are substantial intellectual outputs, it is less likely that they will have been published in an open access environment and therefore the full text of the work may not be available.

While book chapters are a smaller contribution to the whole, there are some concerns from publishers that specialist harvesting techniques may be able to recreate the whole work. This is a rather different concept to journal issues as each article stands alone and is only related to the next one through the decision-making process of the editor rather than being part of a related series of information packages.

- *Description*:
  - all or part of a formally published item, it will stand in its own right.
- *Discipline*:
  - all disciplines.
- *File formats*:
  - text-based.
- *Quality standards*:
  - the publishers of the work will ensure that it meets their quality standards before publishing it.
- *Alternatives to institutional repository*:
  - depending on the discipline there may be subject-based repositories where the full text can be deposited, and many location tools such as library catalogues and online bookshops can be used to locate the item and arrange for a copy to be acquired.

Conference presentations/papers/posters

There are many outputs from conferences and these can vary from the presentation aids used during a talk to a formal refereed paper. The 'formality' of the conference is set by the discipline and organisers.

- *Description*: One or more of
  - speaker's aids for a presentation;
  - poster describing the project;
  - a formal written piece of work.
- *Discipline*:
  - all disciplines, however, it is a more important method of dissemination than journal articles in certain disciplines, such as computer science.

- *File formats*:
  - word-processing formats, presentation graphics formats or even video of the event.
- *Quality standards*:
  - most 'academic' conferences review the submissions, and therefore the intellectual content and the papers which are formally published, although the presentations/posters are not reviewed;
  - for conferences for practitioners, especially those relating to user groups, there is likely to be less, or even no, review of the content; this is especially true where the proceedings are not formally published but put on a user group website.
- *Alternatives to institutional repository*:
  - website for the conference, which may be limited to those who attended or a particular user group;
  - the standard library catalogues for the formal conference proceedings;
  - project or personal websites.

Grey literature

This is material that is not formally published but is released informally. It can be the hardest type of material to locate due to this form.

- *Description*:
  - material that is not formally published and thus can be very hard to track.
- *Discipline*:
  - most.

- *File formats*:
  - mostly text file formats.
- *Quality standards*:
  - no external input to the quality, but may be some internal review.
- *Alternatives to institutional repository*:
  - depending on the context in which the material is produced, it may be available electronically.

Journal article

This entry refers to the finally produced version. The author's rights to deposit this version are dependent on the agreement with the publisher.

- *Description*:
  - this is a piece of text, with associated illustrations, intended to disseminate the results of research; versions before the formally published one may be available, depending on discipline;
  - illustrations can include photographs, diagrams, graphs, output from scientific instruments or output from analytical software packages;
  - formal publishers may be commercial, society or not for profit; they are not normally connected with the author's institution;
  - most publishers assign a digital object identifier (DOI) to formally published articles to uniquely identify the electronic article for the long term, and facilitate retrieval of the publisher's version of the article, subject to licensing rights.

- *Discipline*:
  - all disciplines.
- *File formats*:
  - initial stages may have different components in separate packages but the formally published version is likely to be available as a PDF file.
  - text file formats will include Microsoft Word, Latex, postscript, open source word-processing formats.
- *Quality standards*:
  - a peer-review process of is undertaken for most journals to ensure the work is of appropriate quality.
- *Alternatives to institutional repository*:
  - specialist subject-based repositories such as arXiv for particle physics preprints, Cogprint for psychology or PubMed for medical/biological sciences;
  - access to the publisher's version;
  - access through aggregators and document supply services, for which a fee would be levied.

Preprint

The term refers to any version(s) of the work before any formal publication. This is a loose term and may include alterations following peer-review comments.

- *Description*:
  - this is a piece of text, with associated illustrations, intended to disseminate the results of research; versions before the formally published one may be available, depending on discipline;

- illustrations can include photographs, diagrams, graphs, output from scientific instruments or output from analytical software packages.

- **Discipline:**
  - all disciplines.

- **File formats:**
  - initial stages may have the different components in separate packages but the formally published version is likely to be available as a PDF file.
  - text file formats will include Microsoft Word, Latex, postscript, open source word-processing formats.

- **Quality standards:**
  - it may be unclear as to whether the preprint has undergone any external review.

- **Alternatives to institutional repository:**
  - specialist subject-based repositories such as arXiv for particle physics preprints, Cogprint for psychology or PubMed for medical/biological sciences.

Technical reports and working papers

- **Description:**
  - this is text with associated illustrations, intended to record and disseminate interesting or important technical details which are not suitable for journal publication;
  - these are usually published by the research institution or university of the author;
  - they are likely to be part of a formal series and the unique report number will reflect this.

- *Discipline*:
  - all scientific disciplines.
- *File formats*:
  - initial stages may have the different components in separate packages.
  - text file formats will include Microsoft Word, Latex, postscript, open source word-processing formats.
- *Quality standards*:
  - these will have been put in place by the institution which published it, usually to ensure that the reputation of the organisation is not harmed and that valuable intellectual property is retained.
- *Alternatives to institutional repository*:
  - in particle physics the ArXiv and CERN document server both have technical reports;
  - systems provided by the issuing body.

Theses

- *Description*:
  - this is piece of text with associated illustrations, submitted by the author to a university in order to gain a doctorate or masters degree;
  - illustrations can include photographs, diagrams, graphs, output from scientific instruments or output from analytical software packages;
  - the thesis is not formally published anywhere but will have acknowledgment of both the author and the awarding institution.
- *Discipline*:
  - all disciplines.

- *File formats*:
  - text-based formats such as Word and Latex.
- *Quality standards*:
  - the awarding institution decides whether the thesis is of the appropriate quality for the qualification for which it is being presented.
- *Alternatives to institutional repository*:
  - central services for a particular country or regulating body;
  - many institutions have specialist thesis repositories kept separate from others that contain different material.

Journal article versions and identifying linked versions

As digital objects become freely available from many different locations at more stages in the production process it is becoming more difficult to be able to identify what exactly has been found, who made it available and what the differences are in located versions. Using a location tool such as an internet search engine may find several different versions of a particular article but it can be difficult to establish whether they are the same without looking inside each object retrieved, which is time-consuming.

There are a series of projects and working groups looking into the area of version identification and this section discusses some of the results so far.

One of the main issues is the lack of unambiguous semantics in the different stages of a scholarly work. In this context it is usually journal articles that pose the greatest problems. Figure 4.3 shows the process for journal articles which are formally published with some of the common terms for the versions.

Figure 4.3　**Journal article stages and possible names**

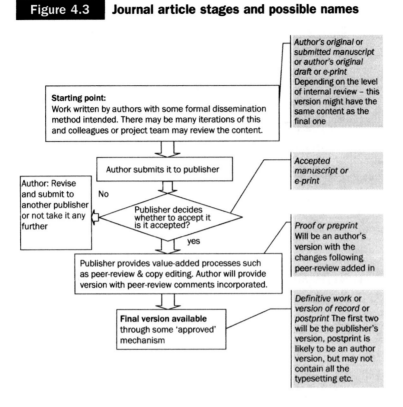

To illustrate this point, consider the following use case:

> Researcher J has an information requirement for a particular topic. She starts by using an internet search engine and retrieves a selection of references. The retrieved set includes some websites and some journal articles. The articles look interesting but then J notices that they all have the same title/authors and are likely to be the same article. The location for this article includes: a publisher's website, two repositories (one subject-based and one institutional) and an author's personal website.

Of course, J may choose a version based on her experiences of the three locations on offer, making implicit and explicit judgments about the quality of the repositories. How important the article is likely to be will also affect the judgments and decisions she makes at this point. However, at present, it will be difficult for J to establish the differences between the versions without inspecting the contents of the file.

Work is underway with respect to the nomenclature and semantics of versions and the rest of this section looks at these. Different approaches to the subject area are described, and it is interesting to compare and contrast them.

CrossRef

CrossRef (*http://www.crossref.org/*) is a membership organisation that is responsible for DOIs in the publisher domain. A DOI is a unique identifier for the electronic version of an article, and the intention is that a particular DOI will always resolve to this electronic copy over time. The DOI is always assigned by CrossRef to the final publisher version. CrossRef has produced a glossary of terms, relating to the publication process and the different stages of nomenclature. The section below picks out some of the most common stages:

- *Accepted work*: The version following significant value-adding activities such as peer review but prior to final typesetting.

- *Author's original draft*: The version deemed ready for reading by others (by the author).

- *Definitive work*: The final version of a work which has been published and should have been assigned a DOI by the publisher.

- *E-print*: Version of work available online which has been submitted or accepted for publication. Encompasses both 'preprint' and 'post-print'. These are excluded from deposit in CrossRef. All versions should contain DOI links to the publisher's definitive version as soon as it is available.

- *Major revision*: Different enough from the definitive work to warrant its own DOI.

- *Original work*: Any work that is fixed in a tangible form of expression can by communicated by machine or device. Such works can be assigned a DOI. Can include literary works, musical works, motion picture, sound recordings etc.

National Information Standards Organisation/Association of Learned and Professional Society Publishers

The National Information Standards Organisation (NISO, *http://www.niso.org*) an international group with representatives of publishers, libraries and other related organisations, and the Association of Learned and Professional and Society Publishers (ALPSP; *http://www .alpsp.org*) have been working together to address the field of article versions.[9] The working group took a lifecycle approach and has identified the following stages in the journal article production process:

- *Author's original*: The version(s) as produced by the author before it starts the publishing process. It may have undergone some internal peer review.

- *Accepted manuscript*: The stage where the content has been accepted by an external party for dissemination.

- *Proof*: Any version where the external party has made corrections, set a house style etc.

- *Version of record*: The version that is accepted as the final one at that point. It is the one that will be preserved for the long term. Although there is only one version of record there may be many copies of this in multiple locations, just as was the case with print journals.

- *Corrected version of record*: Cases where minor mistakes have been found in the version of record and it is corrected for accuracy.

- *Enhanced version of record*: Reflecting items which cannot be represented in print, such as live links to data etc.

The group took the view that the content rather than the file format was important, so there are no references to this. These definitions are similar in scope to the CrossRef ones, but there are variations, for example the differences between accepted work, accepted manuscript and proof.

RIVER project

The RIVER project was a study done for JISC which reported in March 2006.[10] It suggested a typology of versions:

- *Digital copy*: A digital object that is identical to the predecessor object in both content and format.

- *Digital variant*: A digital object that is the same as the predecessor object in content but not format.

- *Digital revision*: A digital object where the content has been modified but the item has not been renamed.

- *Digital edition*: A digital object where the content has evolved from the predecessor.

- *Digital equivalent*: A relationship between two digital objects where there is no formal relationship but they may be functionally equivalent in a certain context.

This concentrates on both the format and the content and the descriptions are not related to the publishing world, unlike the previous two examples.

The study identifies four areas where identification of the version is important:

- being able to distinguish between versions and how these are presented to the end user;
- access and authorisation control;
- digital edition identification;
- workflow.

The main recommendations were for better semantics in this area for clear and consistent communication, identification of workflow management of versions and more guidance for users in this area.

Revisiting the use case using the different terminologies

To revisit our use case, if some of the semantics suggested above were adopted by the community then the situation might be as follows:

> Researcher J has an information requirement for a particular topic. She starts by using an internet search engine and retrieves a selection of references. The retrieved information includes some websites and some journal articles. J notices that the interesting articles all have the same title/authors and are likely to be the same. The location for this article includes: a publisher's website, two repositories (one subject-based and one institutional) and an author's personal website.

This time:

- The publisher's website version is tagged as *version of record*. This explicitly states the implicit assumption in the starting version of this use case. In the RIVER model this would be a *digital edition*.

- The subject repository version is tagged as *e-print*. The author deposited the pre-publication version into this subject repository at the time the article was submitted to the journal as is the practice in the domain where she works. For RIVER this may be a *digital variant* or a *digital revision* depending on content and format changes.

- The institutional repository version is tagged as *version of record*. The journal publisher allows the final PDF to be deposited into the institutional repository and the author has done so, after the end of the embargo period. In RIVER, this would be the same *digital edition* as the final version (so a *digital copy*).

- The personal website version is tagged as *author's original*. The author keeps their CV up to date on their own website and has put up the original version. In RIVER this would be the *original digital object*.

Using this additional information she can chose to view the version which is best for her. It is likely that the publisher's version is the only one where there may be subscription barriers or an invitation to pay to view the article.

The three approaches discussed above show some of the problems in this area. It is difficult to select terminology which is both understandable by the present community but not already overladen with semantic meaning. However, the important issue in this is for researchers to realise that not every version is identical and is the same as the final approved one. It is up to them to decide what the appropriate use decisions are, as long as they understand that there are decisions to be made.

Legal issues

This section gives a brief overview of the legal issues involved in building a repository.

The creator of an intellectual work has certain rights over it, to ensure that their endeavours are rewarded. However, this may not be as straightforward as it sounds as the copyright of the material may belong to the creator's employer through conditions in the contract of employment. In many cases when the item is published the creator will sign a contract with the publisher and may hand over rights to the publisher in recompense for having the work disseminated more widely.

Those rights that are handed over and those that are retained are not standard across the publishing industry and may even vary across titles within a publisher's portfolio. To be able to deposit the full text of the work in an institutional repository, it is important for the author to ensure that they retain the right to do so. Some publishers have the concept of an embargo period where the full text must not be accessible from the repository to the general public; these periods vary from a few months to years. This is to ensure that the publisher's revenue is not damaged by having a freely accessible version available. JISC and SURF have done some work in this area to identify model licences.[11]

The repository managers also need to have rights assigned to them to ensure that they can manage the deposition correctly. It is important to be able to copy and potentially modify the files for long-term management. On[e] important issues to consider is the removal of ite[m] items deposited within the repository are accessible t[o] [all] the repository, the managers have a responsibility to ensure that the content is not libellous or defamatory. There needs to be procedures in place to ensure that this type of content is removed expeditiously.

In the UK, repository content is likely to be covered under database rights which protect the intellectual content and endeavour that went into making the database. As one of the reasons for repositories is to share content and to run additional services on top, some repository owners do not assert this right.

Conclusions

Content and the descriptive metadata that enables the end user to find the content is the most important part of the repository. What content is acceptable is a decision to be taken within the organisational context, but different types of content bring different requirements for description and eventually long-term care and custody. For a successful repository, not only does the metadata need to fulfil the present requirements, but it also needs to be understood and used consistently so that the original meaning would be retained if the content were to be migrated to different software. For more detailed, expert advice, Guenther[12] and Goldsmith and Knudson[13] offer a good next step.

An as-yet unresolved issue to consider is the terminology of journal article versions and how discovering different versions in the research process affects the process itself. In many disciplines, pre-publication versions have been available long before electronic access changed the publishing model. That being so, the fact that it was a different version was more obvious than it is now, even if it is just as difficult to identify the differences between versions.

Finally there are legal issues to address. These have been outlined in this chapter, but for more detailed, expert advice, Knight[14] is a good next step. This is an evolving but murky area and this is not the final endpoint.

Notes

1. IFLA Study Group on the Functional Requirements for Bibliographic Records (1998) 'Functional Requirements for Bibliographic Records', available at: *http://www.ifla.org/VII/ s13/frbr/frbr.pdf* (accessed 2 May 2007).
2. Dublin Core Metadata Initiative (2006) 'Dublin Core Element Set', available at: *http://dublincore.org/documents/dces/* (accessed 2 May 2007).
3. Allinson, J., Johnston, P. and Powell, A. (2007) 'A Dublin Core profile for scholarly works', *Ariadne 50*, available at: *http://www.ariadne.ac.uk/issue50/allinson-et-al/* (accessed 2 May 2007).
4. JISC (2007) 'Scholarly works application profile', available at: *http://www.ukoln.ac.uk/repositories/digirep/index/Eprints_ Application_Profile* (accessed 2 May 2007).
5. Library of Congress (2007) 'MARC standards', available at: *http://www.loc.gov/marc/* (accessed 2 May 2007).
6. Library of Congress (2007) 'Metadata Object Description Schema, available at: *http://www.loc.gov/standards/mods/* (accessed 2 May 2007).
7. World Wide Web Consortium (2007) 'Extensible Markup Language (XML)', available at: *http://www.w3.org/XML/* (accessed 2 May 2007).
8. OAI-PMH (2004) 'The Open Archives Initiative Protocol for Metadata Harvesting', available at: *http://www.openarchives. org/OAI/openarchivesprotocol.html* (accessed 11 April 2007).

9. NISO (2007) 'NISO/ALPSP Working Group on Journal Article Versions', available at: *http://www.niso.org/committees/Journal_versioning/JournalVer_comm.html* (accessed 2 May 2007).

10. Rumsey, S., Shipsey, F., Fraser, M., Noble, H., Bide, M., Look, H. and Kahn, D. (2006) 'Scoping Study on Repository Version Identification (RIVER)', available at: *http://www.jisc.ac.uk/uploaded_documents/RIVER%20Final%20Report.pdf* (accessed 2 May 2007).

11. JISC (2007) 'JISC/SURF partnership on legal matters', available at: *http://www.jisc.ac.uk/whatwedo/projects/programme_jiscsurfipr.aspx* (accessed 14 May 2007).

12. Guenther, R. (2006) 'Standards Showcase: MODS, METS, MARCSML', paper presented at American Library Association Annual Conference, 24–27 June, New Orleans, available at: *http://www.loc.gov/standards/mods/mods-mets-ala/mods-mets-ala.html* (accessed 14 May 2007).

13. Goldsmith, B. and Knudson F. (2006) 'Repository librarian and the next crusade: the search for a common standard for digital repository metadata', *DLib* 12(9), available at: *http://www.dlib.org/dlib/september06/goldsmith/09goldsmith.html* (accessed 14 May 2007).

14. Knight, G. (2004) 'Report on a deposit licence for E-prints', available at: *http://www.sherpa.ac.uk/documents/D4-2_Report_on_a_deposit_licence_for_E-prints.pdf* (accessed 19 July 2007).

5

Curation

Introduction

This chapter discusses the technical and cultural issues involved in ensuring that digital content is available and usable over the long term. As with every area there are discussions about terminology. Two of the most common terms used in this area are *preservation* and *curation*. While these are used fairly interchangeably to imply that the content will be looked after over a considerable period, there is emerging a difference in emphasis and result. The emphasis on curation, for example, implies that not only is the item kept for the long term but it is also usable over the long term. Terms such as *preservation* and *archiving* may carry the assumption that while the item may exist physically (or electronically), it may no longer be usable.

There are two technical aspects in this area, the first being to ensure that the physical item remains intact at the bitstream level and secondly that the digital object remains understandable. Bitstream preservation is a well understood area, as digital storage media, such as discs and tapes, degrade and have to be replaced. For an item to be usable over the long term, meaningful information about it needs to be retained and linked to the item itself; this includes the semantics and operational practicalities on how to use the item. If the semantics are lost, the information cannot be understood, rendering it useless even though it is still functionally usable. An example of semantic loss might be a spreadsheet with columns with no names, or non-unique names such as 'date'. The columns will be meaningful while the spreadsheet remains in use, as the user will know what type of date they refer to. To someone new, it will be unclear whether the date is the creation date, modification date or the date the data was input into the spreadsheet or any of the other possible options. Semantic information can be lost within a short period of time, so ensuring that this is complete and understandable over the long term is a complex job. If the functional instructions are lost, then the tool needed to render the information may not be accessible and the information is also useless. Some of the conceptual models in this domain are very concerned ensuring that the semantics and other information setting the context of the items are captured and curated with the item.

While the content of many systems may last decades, it is not often that long-term curation is considered at the start. For example, some of the electronically-created metadata describing physical library material acquired by the Rutherford Laboratory in the mid-1970s is still available electronically, four library management systems and 30 years later, but the concept that this information would still be available did not inform the original design decisions. These transfers have been possible through a clear understanding of the metadata so that it can be mapped from system to system. In the bibliographic world, standards and conventions, such as MARC[1] and AACR-2[2] ensure that the context and semantics of the metadata are retained, ensuring that as long as the data can be extracted from a library system in a known format, then it can be imported to a new system while retaining its meaning, thus making bibliographic data system-neutral.

However, an integral part of building an institutional repository is an awareness that the information is being collected for the long term. As repositories have digital content as well as metadata then there are more complicated issues to consider. With complex digital objects rather than text-based metadata, preservation and curation issues are more to the front as file formats can last for a couple of years before being replaced with newer versions which are not always backwards-compatible. System-neutral metadata is achievable within institutional repositories although at present there are many standards to choose from; the same does not hold true for complex digital objects. For example, the content within a document is wrapped with the internal information used by the software package that created it to be able to display the formatting. Depending on the package, the content may not be accessible without the software used to make the document as the wrapper is produced using proprietary standards limited to one software company. Each new version of the software brings additional problems as the documents created in one version may not be usable in another as the wrapper changes. This makes curation of this type of information more complicated. The more complex and the more specialised the tool used to generate the information, the more complex the technical curation issues are.

There are not just technical issues in this field; one of the most important strategic and cultural issues is exactly what should be curated for the long term. This encompasses collection management decisions on what is to be curated and how it is to be curated. Is the whole collection to be kept for the long term, or are some parts more important than others? What level of preservation is going to be attempted: is it the complete item with the look and feel as it was originally created, or is it just the content of the item so that the look and feel may not be preserved? Ensuring the look and feel is preserved can be more complicated but might bring benefits in the long term. These benefits may not be for the designated community but for unforeseen reuse. For example, these can be in sociological research in the future – old adverts in newspapers can be as interesting today as the original articles were originally. This leads to a need to understand who the information is being preserved for, in the first instance. Knowing the intended audience will help decide what level of additional information is needed to ensure that the item is understandable and usable over its lifetime. Finally, what are the resourcing implications and how will they be supported over the longer term?

Curation, as with every area, has its own specialist terms. One of the common terms used in this area is *ingest*, which is the process of adding the information into the repository – not just the fact of a new entry, but also any processes required to ensure the first stage of archiving. *Fixity* records if and when an object has been modified; this is a vital part of verification and audit trails of changes. *Registry* is used to denote a centrally kept service where information such as file formats can be looked up. This minimises the work need for each repository and standardises the results. The National Archives PRONOM service (*http://www .nationalarchives.gov.uk/pronom/*) is an example of this. The Open Archival Information System (OAIS) model also relies on registries.[3] *Render* is the act of showing the file in the original form as it was intended to be. It implies that some special actions have taken place beyond starting up the application that generated the object in the first place.

This chapter discusses some basic concepts and what additional metadata might be required and looks at some of the current work in this area.

Cultural issues

To return to the theme of the stakeholders discussed in Chapter 2, what particular issues are there for them?

One of the common themes in curation is to define the audience or end users. This is often referred to as the *designated community*. This designated community is expected to have some knowledge of the subject under discussion rather than simply representing the general public. This makes the additional semantic information required more straightforward as it can be less explicit than what is required for someone with no knowledge of the subject area. While this is a good and useful starting point, archive material is sometimes used for an entirely different purpose than originally envisaged. An example of this is using National Archives data on passengers on nineteenth-century ships for genealogical purposes. However, as it would be impossible to store all the implicit and explicit information on objects for unknown reuse, the identification and documentation of designated communities becomes an essential part of curation. It may be difficult to identify future end users of the information and their needs as, by the nature of the exercise, they are still in the future. However, it is a certainty that they will want to know that the information has not been damaged by the passage of time or, if it has, to be able to ascertain what effect this has had on its integrity. There will be some interest in the provenance of the object as this is a vital part in deciding its quality and worth.

There are also cultural issues to identify for the depositing authors. What are their expectations of the institutional repository? Is there anything in the deposition agreement that gives guidance about the longevity of the information? Will they make different decisions regarding their personal records depending on the policy of the repository or will they think that if the organisation is providing the service, then the information deposited is automatically saved for the long term? Assumptions about the longevity of the ingested information will inform their behaviour. At present, if the work is a journal article then the responsibility of maintaining it over the long term is shared between the journal publisher and the national library, if applicable. Print archiving is more straightforward than electronic archiving, and if the publisher ceases to exist, it is easier for others to take over the archive. This reliance and understanding of the status quo means that researchers are confident that they will be able to retrieve copies of their works from these third parties and do not always ensure that they have access to personal copies of the final article. If this changes significantly then authors may expect that the replacement systems, including institutional repositories will provide the same service.

Some information providers, such as publishers and national libraries, already have preservation in their remit. Companies such as Elsevier Publishing are joining with their national library to preserve the electronic versions of their journals.[4] While national libraries, such as the British Library, were designed as a preservation mechanism for some material, this is less likely to happen for institutional repository content as the present system is predicated on the deposited material having being published. If the publishing paradigm changes then there may be grey areas. However, national libraries may start to offer preservation services for other organisations.

An institution's libraries preservation remit will depend on the collection and remit that they maintain. While there are different skills and requirements for digital preservation, the policy remains the same.

For some information mediators the only effect of preservation is that the information will be there for longer. For institutions and, in some case funders, however, there may be financial implications as preservation activities need underpinning resources to be able to function correctly over the long term. It is therefore important to ensure that these resource implications are considered.

Policy, management and resourcing issues

There are policy and management decisions with any collection, physical or electronic. The three most obvious ones are: what should be added to the collection, which has already been dealt with in previous chapters; what, if anything, should leave the collection, and what resources are required to maintain the collection. These decisions are not made in isolation; stakeholders in this process include the end users of the service and the senior management of the organisation. End users are interested in being able to satisfy their information requirements as quickly and efficiently as possible, while senior management will be interested in the costs and benefits of the service provided. Balancing the needs of the stakeholders against the resourcing required is a vital part of successful collection management. Depending on the age of the collection, different facets of this management process are at the forefront of the manager's mind. However, as managing digital assets over many years takes more intervention and resources than managing print ones, then it is recommended that all aspects of the collection development policy should be considered at or near the start of the collection.

Considering the issue of what might leave a collection and the factors that might influence the decision, there are two ways of identifying items for withdrawal from a collection: at the point where the item is collected, equivalent to a retention schedule in an archive, or secondly at some point later in the life of the item. There are many reasons why retention and withdrawal decisions might be made later in the item's lifecycle, including:

- obsolete information: the content of the item is no longer fit for purpose – this is particularly true in fast-moving areas such as computing or electronics;
- damaged beyond repair;
- collection no longer required to cover this material: collection remit has altered as a result of organisational change.

While these reasons for considering removing an item from the collection are valid, they go hand in hand with other considerations. For example, if damaged materials are still required is it possible to get an alternative? Does the holding library have any responsibilities to keep the material? For example, the material may have been published by the organisation, such as technical reports, or the item may have historical significance to the organisation, or the organisation may have agreed to keep the item/collection for a third party following a donation or even a legally binding contract. There will also be policy guidelines to follow. Balancing these competing needs, the removal decisions can be made.

All these policy and retention/withdrawal decisions are relevant to the digital information held in an institutional repository, albeit more opaquely, as the digital objects are not as visible as physical items on shelves, making the issue more complicated. As the remit of the system is to collect the output of the organisation, the content is not going to fall out of the scope of the collection while the organisation is still in existence. The intellectual content within a particular item may become technically obsolete, but the item itself has historic value for the organisation as part of the metrics. The equivalent of 'damaged beyond repair' is still true. Digital objects can get corrupted or, if not managed, can become stuck in an obsolete format. In this case it is likely that the associated metadata would remain usable and the decision would concern whether having the object itself was important. Depending on the item in question, it might be possible to get the item from elsewhere. The cost-benefit analysis might tip in either direction. If curation is an active decision from the start, then conscious decisions may be made at the outset that items are not going to be curated for the long term.

These decisions might not apply to the whole collection within the institutional repository. Depending on what type of information the institutional repository holds, there may be different levels of importance over what should be curated and what is acceptable to 'lose'. There should also be the realisation that it may not be possible to curate everything and thus a 'pecking order' of importance may be useful to establish. Taking the material types discussed in the last chapter, one can see that there are different perceptions of academic and organisational worth which do not necessarily run along the same lines (Table 5.1).

It would be an effective policy to consider and document the retention and preservation decisions for the different material types when producing the policy for the institutional repository.

A physical collection management process can still be applied to the digital collection. As well as adding and removing items from the collection, there are management

Table 5.1 Types of materials held in repositories and potential alternative locations

Material type	Comments
Books and book chapters	This will be published elsewhere. For traditional books, the archival mechanism is still print. Electronic books is still a developing area and these preservation and curation issues have not been resolved.
Conference papers/presentations/ posters	Some of this may be published elsewhere. These may be in forms which are difficult to preserve. The look and feel of presentations are an important part of the experience.
Grey literature	By definition this is not published elsewhere. It may be of importance locally even if not of greater importance.
Journal articles	If the article has been published in a formal journal, then it will be preserved by the journal publisher. However this may not be accessible to the users of the particular institutional repository.
Preprints	Preprints in the print world were a mechanism to ensure rapid dissemination of important new discoveries, which were then formally documented in the journal literature. With the advent of preprint archives such as ArXiv, these are more obviously available for long periods of time.
Technical reports and working papers	These are likely to have been published by the organisation that owns the institutional repository and thus they may have some responsibility to ensure that this information is available for the long term or there may be organisational archiving and disposal policies in place.
Theses	While there is the responsibility of the approving organisation to keep these, there are also many national initiatives to collect all the electronic theses in one place.

tasks such as looking for damaged items and stock-taking to ensure that what is recorded as being present still exists. These types of activities should be done for digital repositories and are pointed to in the Open Archival Information System (OAIS) as management processes. To be able to identify damaged items, it is important to be able to identify what the original state was. This could be done by processes such as checksums or file comparisons as well as trying to render the files. This type of active collection management requires resources and technical expertise and shows the importance of deciding on the longevity of the collection before embarking on this type of activity.

The type of collection management described above usually sits on a firm base of policy, an understanding of the purpose of the collection and for whom it is intended. It is therefore important for a repository to have the same understanding for its collection and users, especially for resource management.

Collection management in any form has resourcing implications, staff, equipment and money, and for good budget management these requirements need to be identified. Although the costs for physical preservation are well understood, this is not true for electronic collections. As curation of large digital collections is still in the research phase, it is difficult to be certain about identifying the resourcing issues involved. There are many approaches to how one might estimate the costs and an obvious one is to look at the different collection management phases. The LIFE project (*http://www.ucl.ac.uk/ls/life/*) has taken this approach and has produced some methods for quantifying the different stages. The stages are:

- *Acquisition*: the costs of acquiring the information. The model considers all types of electronic material, including resources that would incur a purchase cost. This cost is likely to be low or zero for institutional repositories. What costs there are for this phase diminish as a proportion of the whole over time as they are fixed at the point of acquisition.

- *Ingest*: This covers the quality assurance and deposit cycle. How the material is put into the system and what checks are made to ensure that the physical deposit has worked correctly and that the item is undamaged by the process.

- *Metadata*: Ensuring the correct metadata is associated with the item. This is ensuring that the metadata is input and is correct. For the initial examples used in the LIFE model, the systems concerned did not have self-deposit as an option.

- *Access*: Ensuring that the item was locatable and accessible to the right people over the long term.

- *Storage*: Looking after the bits and bytes to ensure preservation at the most basic level.

- *Preservation*: Doing the planning, checking and preservation actions needed to ensure long-term preservation.

It is interesting to see how well these concepts map both into the OAIS model and the activities outlined in the trusted repository criteria discussed elsewhere in this chapter. The LIFE project concluded that the major costs of this activity are linked to the preservation tools needed to perform the preservation activity. The ingest and metadata stages for information put into an institutional repository may be harder to quantify as they are distributed to the creator of the material whereas the other stages are likely to be done by the repository managers. To decide whether to include the time spent by people who are not directly involved in managing the repository would then depend on the scope of the resourcing question.

The outcomes of this project can be generalised as although the price per object may not be a lot of money, the overall costs are quite great. There is research in the area of preservation of institutional repositories. Two UK-based projects are SHERPA-DP (*http://www.sherpadp.org.uk/*) and PRESERV (*http://preserv.eprints.org/*). Although they take a different approach, what is interesting is the common belief that a repository may want to outsource the preservation aspects to a specialist service, thus putting the expertise in one (or a few) places and being able to share the costs and benefits. This replicates what happens in the print world, where specialist services such as national libraries have a remit to preserve in perpetuity. These types of services are not yet widely available, and there remains the question about how outsourcing the preservation aspects of a repository would impact on trusted repository certification.

There are several organisations whose remit is to provide support and advice in the preservation world. They include the Digital Curation Centre (*http://www.dcc.ac.uk/*) in the UK, the Digital Preservation Coalition (*http://www .dpconline.org/*), and the National Digital Information Infrastructure and Preservation Programme (*http://www .digitalpreservation.gov/*) in the USA; information on international partners is also available.[5]

Open Archival Information System model

OAIS is a conceptual model to ensure that data repository archival needs are considered. It has come out of the space data community, but is now applied in other areas rather than science data repositories and is an ISO standard (ISO 14721).

The basic underlying principle is that 'representation information' must be applied for a particular data object to be meaningful and usable in a particular context.

Such representation information attempts to describe all the information required to render the content in a meaningful way to a designated community. This is an important point as it makes the assumption that the people who will be attempting to reuse the data are from a fixed set or community with domain expertise. This may not address the problems of when the domain alters and what an expert can be expected to know in decades or even longer from now.

The OAIS model uses a concept of information packages. It defines three types of package, varying according to their functional use:

- *Submission information package (SIP)*: This is generated as the item is ingested in the repository. There is not necessarily a one-to-one relationship with archival information packages (AIPs). Many SIPs can make up an AIP; however, the packaging information will always be present.

- *Archival information package (AIP)*: This is the preservation entity and as such should contain all the information needed to be able to preserve the content for the long term.

- *Dissemination information package (DIP)*: This is produced by the repository from one or more AIPs in response to a user request for information.

For every type of information package, there are two types of entity: the *content information* and the *preservation description information (PDI)*. To be able to generate the PDI, the content information must be fully understood and the representation information generated. Representation information will need to cover both the structure of the data object and the semantic meaning so that the data object is understandable. With this type of information it will be possible to render the bitstream into the data object. This representation information can be a recursive structure so that the representation information may need its own representation information to be understandable. This relationship continues until the base item is at a level considered to be basic knowledge for the designated community. The potential end of this recursion is information in a printed format. Some of this representation information may not be kept locally but be part of a national or internal registry. An example of this might be information on file formats which are not unique to a particular project but are common to everyone trying to preserve and curate digital files.

The PDI covers the provenance of the content information, context, reference to unique identifiers of the content and finally fixity to provide a mechanism for identifying unauthorised changes. This information enables an audit of changes to be kept so that a future user can ascertain how reliable and undamaged the material was and to make decisions as appropriate.

The packing information links the content to the PDI. Associated with it is the descriptive information about this package so that it can be located and used.

Associated with the concepts related to the information, there are a series of processes to be considered and planned:

- *Ingest*: This process manages the submission, both physical and at a policy level, of content and the generation of archival quality information and the AIP. It will perform the necessary verification and validation checks on the input and record information within the system.

- *Data management*: This manages the underlying database which manages the system, ensuring that the structure (schema) is correct and also runs any queries needed to retrieve information.

- *Archival storage*: Provides the ability to store, maintain and retrieve the AIPs.

- *Access*: Supporting the consumers of the repository to be able to retrieve the information and use it, this process generates DIPs.

- *Preservation planning*: Monitoring the environment and providing recommendations to ensure that this remains suitable, this includes both technical facets and user requirements. Migration planning is also part of this role.

- *Administration*: Manages the policies for ingest. Provides reporting tools and documents processes and systems.

This standard is a conceptual model and as such does not prescribe any technical details of how it is to be implemented. It does give a framework for ensuring that the archival needs are considered from the start and separates the requirements for archival information from the submission and dissemination processes.

The standard is in the middle of a standard five-year review in late 2006/early 2007 and the updates coming from this process are not yet known.

Trusted repositories

The Research Libraries Group (*http://www.rlg.org/*) and the American National Archives and Records Administration (*http://www.archives.gov/*) are working on the concept of digital repository certification to be able to build up a network of trusted repositories.[6]

The Research Libraries Group is intending to create an audit and certification process so that standards can be identified and repositories tested against them. The areas the criteria cover are part of good project and system management and are likely to have been identified and considered during the repository set-up planning stages. This piece of work is built on the OAIS model and uses some of the same terminology.

All information discovery and use of the resulting resources are underpinned by personal decisions on relevance and trustworthiness of the material located. This may lead to unconscious preferences when selecting from a list of possible resources to use. As repositories populated by end users are a relatively new phenomenon, having a formal external certification process may aid users to decide on the relevance of the information contained within the service located. It will also help those organisations that may be building services on top of repositories to decide whether the underlying repository is managed to the level that is acceptable to be included in their service.

The criteria fall into four areas. As these focus on different areas of repository management and service delivery, they may be the responsibility of different parts of the support team.

Organisation

This examines areas such as whether the organisation itself is governed well and is viable in the long term. It looks to ensure that the repository has policies, procedures and contracts in place to ensure longevity of the repository and the information contained within it. It also ensures that reliability and accountability of the operation of the archive is taken seriously. Part of this remit is to ensure that the staffing level is appropriate and that staff are fully trained. These issues could be summed up by the term *good governance*.

Repository functions, processes and procedures

This is looking at how the content is gained, what policies and strategies are in place and how the planning for the preservation of the content has been done. For the ingest process, there must be clear and documented understanding of what is acceptable content, the ability to have the rights to preserve the information effectively documented and a clear verification process to ensure that the ingest procedure has not corrupted anything. Once the ingest process is completed an AIP should be generated. To be able to ensure the archival process continues there should be clear documentation outlining the definitions of acceptable AIPs and how these are derived from the ingest process together with a verification process. The next strand in this area is a documented understanding of the preservation planning strategies implemented in the repository. The repository must be able to show good data management, thus providing the links between the AIP and the ability to use it. Finally in this area there are criteria linked to the subject of access management. This not only includes ensuring the correct levels of access but the ability to monitor 'access denial' situations. It also concerns the documentation of the procedure to generate a DIP.

The designated community and the usability of the information

For successful preservation, assumptions need to be made about who is going to use this information, i.e. the designated community. The decision about who they are needs to be documented. Congruent with this is an appreciation of the metadata required by the community to use the repository effectively. Policies about access and delivery options should be in place and accessible by the designated community; this can be likened to a service level agreement. However, the criteria acknowledge that this formal method may not be appropriate for the smaller repository. Having made decisions regarding the designated community and how well they understand the information, it is important to have a process in place to verify that these assumptions are indeed correct.

Technologies and technical infrastructure

To be able to provide a reliable service, the system infrastructure needs to be reliable and well documented. It also needs to have systems in replace to detect corruption and to ensure that these fall within the acceptable limits laid out in the preservation policy. Other parts of this area include good systems management procedures for upgrades, changes and data migration. The repository management should have in place appropriate technology watch procedures to ensure that the repository keeps in step with its designated community. Finally, the security arrangements should be appropriate – this area is closer to business continuity planning rather than just IT security as the management team need to plan and mitigate for physical as well as electronic risks.

Technical issues

From a technical point of view there are four basic approaches to ensuring that a particular item is usable over the long term: initial preservation activity at ingest; keeping watch on the changes in technology and performing a preservation activity when necessary; keeping enough information to be able to mimic the original environment; or preserving the original environment. These all have risks and benefits associated with them.

It is useful to note that the version which is preserved may not be the same as the version which is delivered as part of a dissemination process. This may be a result of the preservation decisions or for the safety of duplication. A number of approaches are given below.

Migrate to start with

This method entails performing some action on the deposited object to enhance the possibility of curation. One example is to convert the deposited objects into a predefined format from which it is considered easier to migrate. For documents, this might be a format such as PDF-A,[7] so that the look and feel is kept, or it might entail translating the content into XML.[8] In either case, there is the decision whether to keep the original deposited item as well as the new version. There are several reasons why one might do this: the original format might prove to be easier to migrate from in the long run, it may be policy to keep the original as well as the alternative version, or it might be in a better format for dissemination. There is also the decision as to whether the archival quality version is going to be the same as the dissemination copy.

Taking this approach requires sufficient resources, staff and infrastructure to support this activity, especially as the initial ingest phase will be more resource-intensive. Although policies will have been fully considered and documented, careful thought needs to be taken in regard to the choice of format into which everything is converted, as this too will eventually need to be migrated to a new format.

From this point on, the usual technology watch and checking processes will continue as in the other methods.

Migrate when necessary

This assumes that the archival version is not migrated to a new format on ingest. In this case there needs to be procedures and processes to identify the different file types deposited and then a technology watch to check that the format is not becoming obsolete.

If a format is identified as obsolete then migration procedures need to be put into action to update the version and associated metadata appropriately.

Emulation

This approach uses emulation of the original hardware and software environment to access the information. Depending on the complexity and uniqueness of the object being held it may be the right way to go.

Preservation of the environment

This approach requires that the original hardware and software used to produce the data is retained in a working state so that the data can be used as it was created. While this might be appropriate for complex data, it is not a realistic approach to the type of information contained within an institutional repository.

Preservation metadata

If curation is one of the aims of the repository, then the metadata required to support this must be included. This section looks at various approaches to this area.

PREMIS

The PREMIS model and associated Data Dictionary are produced by a working group sponsored by OCLC (*http://www.oclc.org/*) and the Research Library Group (RLG). The model builds on the OAIS reference model.[9]

The PREMIS model has five entities: intellectual entities, objects, events, agents and rights. An intellectual entity may be made up of one or more objects. These objects will have rights associated with them to be able to control access and permissions and events, which can be preservation actions. Both rights and events are linked to agents which are people, organisations or automated software. The Data Dictionary considers the metadata that will be required. The following is an overview of the areas suggested:

- *Identifiers*: It must be possible to uniquely identify the objects.

- *Preservation level*: If the repository aims to curate items to different precisions, then this should be recorded.

- *Technical information on the item*: This describes whether the files are encoded, some measure of fixity, the size of the file, the version of the format etc. This can either be captured within the record or be a pointer to a registry of format types such as the UK National Archives PRONOM service.

- *Information relevant to this particular item*: This includes such as properties of the item that need to be preserved for the action to be meaningful, in addition to any potential problems

- *Creating application*: This includes information about the creating application and the dates that the files were generated. This is another area where a registry would be useful.

- *Original name.*

- *Content location within the storage system.*

- *Environment needed to access the content*: Describes what hardware and software will be required to be able to use the file without any further actions.

- *Digital signature*: If the repository uses a digital signature for deposit or for the agreements, then this needs to be recorded together with information on how to check it.

- *Relationship with other content*: A particular entity may be related to other content in the repository: it may be a different version or the same version in a different format. These links are useful to record. For an intellectual entity rendered in many files, such as a digitised version of a printed work, it is important to record the order of the files so that the final work can be rendered in the right order.

- *Events*: For events/actions on the content of the repository there should be an audit trail.

- *Agents*: The repository needs to know who the agents are.

- *Rights and permissions*: This should record what permissions and rights have been given to the repository and its agents.

Comparing these requirements with basic Dublin Core or even MARC cataloguing, it can be seen that many technical details are required. This is an example of the representation and preservation description information discussed in the section about OAIS.

Metadata encoding and transmission standard

METS, from the Library of Congress[10] is designed to provide a standard XML format for transmission of digital library objects between systems. It provides a mechanism for the information packages referred to in the OAIS model. This has a series of sets of metadata to help describe the object:

- *Header describing the METS encoding* not the digital object. This includes information on creation of the METS record and the agent responsible for creating it. The role of the agent is chosen from a fixed set of values: creator, editor, archivist, preservation, disseminator, custodian, IP owner and other. From this, one can see the wide range of roles that have been considered and how complex an environment METS can describe effectively.

- *Descriptive metadata* about the items in the METS object. This can be a pointer to another location. It can contain metadata in other known formats and these can be identified by the use of a special tag.

- *Administrative metadata* has four sections: technical, intellectual property rights, source and digital provenance. This enables the METS record to capture the preservation description information described in the OAIS model.

- *File metadata* about all the files used to generate the digital object.

- *Structural map.* This allows for the record to describe the relationships between different digital objects which may make up the whole logical entity. An example of this might be where a book comprises of a file per chapter, and there needs to be some external information to be able to regroup the different files in the correct order to retrieve the book as a single item.

- *Structural linking* allows for the recording of links within the content held in a METS record.

- *Behaviour metadata* which allows for the description of the systems that need to be used to render the information again.

METS is a complicated standard to interpret if one is not accustomed to using XML. However, it does give a formal structure for transferring information between systems and ensuring that more than just the descriptive metadata is transferred.

These two standards help to implement the abstract concepts held within the OAIS model and the additional information required to be able to ensure preservation of material for the long term.

Conclusions

Although this chapter has discussed preservation with approaches from many different areas, there are many overlapping themes. To be able to decide on the most appropriate processes and procedures it is important to understand what and for whom the repository is undertaking preservation actions. Making conscious decisions about what is to be preserved and making this clear to the designated community is always useful, if tricky. If these issues are clear from the start, this will guide the resourcing and management issues. Having preservation policy in place from the start ensures that the information kept is fit for purpose and there is no need to retro-fit unnecessarily to an existing system. As the area of preservation and curation for institutional repositories is so new, many are concentrating on gaining content rather than long-term issues. As such it is likely that existing repositories will need enhancements for long-term use as preservation requirements become more obvious. It will be interesting to see whether new functions for preservation become widespread, and who performs them. The key is to be aware of the requirements and to keep watch on this area.

Notes

1. Library of Congress (2007) 'MARC standards', available at: *http://www.loc.gov/marc/* (accessed 11 April 2007).
2. American Library Association, the Canadian Library Association, and the Chartered Institute of Library and Information Professionals (2006) 'Anglo-American Cataloguing Rules', available at: *http://www.aacr2.org/* (accessed 11 April 2007).
3. Consultative Committee for Space Data Systems (2002) 'Reference Model for Open Archival Information System', available at: *http://public.ccsds.org/publi-cations/archive/ 650x0b1.pdf* (accessed 11 April 2007).
4. Elsevier (2003) 'Elsevier and Koninklijke Bibliotheek finalise major archiving agreement', available at: *http://www.elsevier.com/ wps/find/authored_newsitem.cws_home/companynews05_ 00020* (accessed 11 April 2007).
5. Library of Congress (year unknown) 'Preservation partners', available at: *http://www.digitalpreservation.gov/partners/alliances. html* (accessed 20 April 2007).
6. RLG (2006) 'Digital Repository Certification', available at: *http://www.rlg.org/en/page.php?Page_ID=580* (accessed 11 April 2007).
7. Adobe (2002) 'PDF as an archiving standard', available at: *http://www.adobe.com/enterprise/pdfs/pdfarchiving.pdf* (accessed 20 April 2007).
8. World Wide Web Consortium (2007) 'Extensible Markup Language (XML)', available at: *http:// www.w3.org/XML/* (accessed 11 April 2007).
9. Library of Congress (2007) 'PREMIS: preservation metadata maintenance activity', available at: *http://www.loc .gov/standards/premis/* (accessed 11 April 2007).
10. Library of Congress (2007) 'METS: metadata encoding and transmission standards', available at: *http://www.loc.gov/ standards/mets/* (accessed 11 April 2007).

6

Experiences

Introduction

This chapter examines the experiences of three different repository building projects. It addresses issues from the local reason for building a repository to the choices made and examines the barriers and successes in getting acceptance and content. The format of this chapter is a case study on each of the repositories followed by some general conclusions. To make the comparisons and contrasts easier, each repository manager was asked the same ten questions; these are repeated in the text. The repositories are taken in alphabetical order.

The repositories chosen are ePubs at the Council for the Central Laboratory of the Research Councils (CCLRC), Cranfield QUEprints at Cranfield University, both in the UK, and the University of Otago in New Zealand. ePubs is the one that I am responsible for and it is an example of a research repository not based in a university. Cranfield University was chosen as it reached 1,000 full-text entries in September 2006 and there is some subject overlap with CCLRC. The University of Otago is the first live New Zealand repository and has some interesting future directions. I would like to thank Simon Bevan from Cranfield University and Graham McGregor, Nigel Stanger and Monica Ballantine from the University of Otago for their help in compiling the case studies.

Although this book is deliberately agnostic about which particular software to use when building an institutional repository, this chapter will include some discussion of the software decisions made as they form part of the project development and expertise of those who have built repositories. The three case studies include DSpace (*http:// www.dspace.org/*) and GNU EPrints (*http://www.eprints.org/*), two of the main market leaders, together with an internal solution.

Council for the Central Laboratory of the Research Councils, UK

About the organisation – what does it do and what type of material is produced

The CCLRC is one of the eight UK Research Councils and consists of three sites: Chilbolton Observatory in Hampshire, Daresbury Laboratory in Cheshire and Rutherford Appleton Laboratory in Oxfordshire. In April 2007 it merged with the Particle Physics and Astronomy Research Council to form the Science and Technology Facility Council. The constituent parts were formed in 1967, 1957 and 1962 respectively. At present there are approximately 1,800 members of staff at the laboratories.

The CCLRC was unique in being the only UK Research Council with no grant-giving function. Rather, it was there to provide large-scale scientific facilities for UK researchers and beyond. These facilities are highly specialised and expensive so that other comparable resources are only found outside the UK. As well as providing specialised support, the CCLRC staff also undertake research in their own right. The subject areas covered are wide but all relate to physical sciences.

Journal articles represent the biggest type of material produced. There are also a large number of conference presentations with associated material. There is a library and information service and the greatest proportion of the budget is spent on scientific journals. Historically, CCLRC has produced a range of technical reports, which are formally published by CCLRC (and its predecessors). These date back to the late 1950s when the National Institute for Research into Nuclear Science was first opened.

One of the unique features of CCLRC's mission is that facility users, rather than CCLRC staff are responsible for most of the science research work, and hence publications, generated from the facilities. So when looking at publications for performance indicators, the net is spread wider than just CCLRC employees. The original remit for the repository was to collect the scientific and technical output of CCLRC.

What were the previous processes for material collection

Many processes for collecting the scientific output have existed during the existence of the organisation. In the recent past, departments had extensive, but different, procedures in place to collect bibliographic references. These procedures included contacting users of the facilities to find out what publications had resulted from use of the facilities. Some funding mechanisms also required individual departments to produce bibliographies for performance monitoring. This federated approach meant that it was difficult to assess the output of the entire organisation as a whole.

What was the impetus to start your institutional repository

In 2002 the Library Committee, who have oversight and governance responsibilities for the CCLRC Library and Information Services, were concerned about the lack of a coherent overall picture of CCLRC outputs together with an interest in ensuring the quality of the output of CCLRC in a more formal method. This resulted in a paper to the internal governing body recommending that the Library and Information Services perform a feasibility study to gauge the need for an 'e-publications archive'.

This feasibility study was undertaken in spring 2003 and it consulted a wide range of potential stakeholders in the process. The main conclusions were:

- there was a perceived need for a single location for the output of CCLRC;
- that an automated mechanism for publication approval prior to publication would be culturally difficult to implement;
- that the science done in the departments with facilities was the most important thing, rather than the organisation of the author;
- at the time there was no external product which could meet the requirements of the organisation;
- further resources, both in staff and equipment were needed to take the project further;
- it was important to be able to link to internal procedures such as annual reporting and the internal people system;
- it was important to find selling points to encourage authors themselves to self-deposit.

Over the next year, a system was written in-house to satisfy the needs of the organisation. The system is conceptually based on Functional Requirements for Bibliographic Records (FRBR)[1] as the concepts of linked material was deemed important in our domain. The ability to link material together to reduce the number of records retrieved is useful, especially in areas, such as particle physics, with a strong preprinting culture. It can also paint a picture of how research work is disseminated and altered for the different forms of dissemination. See Jones and Mascord for further reading on this area.[2]

The ePublications archive went live externally in May 2004 and was affectionately shortened to ePubs soon afterwards. There was some debate within the team about whether ePubs was a suitable name for our repository, but as with most nicknames it was well established with internal name recognition. It is short and snappy and isn't an acronym and in the end we decided to stay with it. In retrospect, maybe we should have thought about the name of the service before we actually did.

ePubs was always designed to hold full text, however, the main focus organisationally is the bibliographic reference. As the open access debate has raised the profile of the issues involved and CCLRC has participated in the RCUK framework on open access so the deposit of full text has become more important. However, there will always be some bibliographic records without full text. This is because much of CCLRC's scientific output is done by authors who are not employed by CCLRC, and although our remit is to collect all of CCLRC's scientific output, we are not grant providers and so cannot mandate the deposit in our institutional repository.

Brief description of the process

The ability to input into the system is determined by the internal user ID account. Any member of staff can input their information and upload the full text. The record is then queued and a member of library staff does some bibliographic checks on it. This ensures that if the full text is uploaded it will comply with legal restrictions using the SHERPA RoMEO resource (*http://www.sherpa.ac.uk/romeo.php*). There are a small but keen set of users who do input metadata and the associated full text. Most of the metadata input is through users who are set up with administrative privileges, whose records appear immediately in ePubs. These users usually have some form of departmental responsibility for publication collection and, on the whole, are not as interested in adding full text as individual authors are.

A suite of checking programs enables library staff to perform validation and verification checks on this type of information. As ePubs allows the user to put a minimal amount of information in, this checking is important.

The most important checks are for:

- empty fields;
- duplicates;
- journal titles.

ePubs holds a validated list of journal titles for the user to choose from, but also allows the user to put new ones in. Sometimes the user does not choose from the list, however, thereby introducing duplicate journal title entries.

Part of the ePubs input process is the ability to link the record to the institution's internal people information system. This means that authors who are inconsistent about how their name is used have all their forms grouped under the same heading in an author index. The actual metadata record has the information as it appeared in the publication for accuracy but it is easier to locate the complete publishing record of a particular author.

Resourcing

The initial feasibility study was funded by the Laboratory Management Board, the rest of the development and support for the institutional repository has come through the budget for library and information services. As a library service we are heavily dependent on journals, and so we are conscious that changes in the journal publishing industry will have a large impact on the way we work. It is therefore strategically important for us to lead the way internally with the institutional repository. Having made this strategic decision we have adjusted our budget to take account of the resourcing implications of the institutional repository. The budget has not been increased, but spending priorities have been amended and ePubs activities presently represent 5 per cent of the total budget, compared with journal subscriptions at just over 50 per cent. The library staff involved in this project were either responsible for IT developments and ePubs fell within their remit, or have had their duties adjusted to take account of the skills required. This readjustment has been possible through consideration of business processes and changing requirements as the service focus shifted away from physical material handling to electronic delivery to the desktop.

Our 2006–2010 strategy document positions the institutional repository at the centre of the service and thus we are committed to resourcing over this timescale.

Approach to curation of the material

At present the curation of the material is still under discussion. There is a project to digitise the full set of technical reports as these are still of scientific interest and, as the issuing organisation, we have a responsibility to curate them. For the print copies we have chosen two techniques: binding a complete set and having multiple copies in different locations. The costs of this form of curation are well understood and are linked to the physical environment. The digitisation project aims to investigate the curation issues relating to electronic versions. This project is also helped by the fact that the organisation owns the copyright of the material and so there are no legal problems to overcome.

Most of the rest of the material is formally published elsewhere and so no formal preservation policy is in place.

Barriers and issues

- *Finding the right tactic to persuade active scientists to use a corporate system.* By the nature of their work, scientists can be reluctant to use centrally provided systems as they feel that they can do better and have better things to do with their time. The ability to rank authors within ePubs by the quantity of publication, while not something that we have publicised has been a factor in some people depositing information.

- *Level of metadata/material awareness.* The downside of having author or near-author input is the fact that they are not trained to catalogue items and may not understand terminology. An interesting thing to enter into the system is a paper from a conference proceedings which is published in book format. Authors are likely to enter this as a chapter or section of a book while a librarian is more likely to designate it as conference proceedings with the bibliographic details of a book.

- *Authors being prepared to enter any metadata at all.* One of the issues currently being addressed is the amount of metadata fields that the authors are prepared to see within the user input workflow. Even if most of them are not mandatory, the very fact that they are present is off-putting. It has been suggested that providing an Excel spreadsheet for upload would be easier. This must be something to do with the familiarity of the system as the amount of keying is exactly the same, although this shows an appreciation of the benefits of a repository.

- *Authors keeping versions which are allowed to be deposited.* In 2005 we undertook an exercise to increase the level of full-text entries by approaching a small group of popular authors within the organisation with a view to offering support to input the full text. This was not particularly successful as we soon discovered that most of our authors do not keep pre-publication versions of articles, instead using the final published version as their record. This came as a surprise to the librarians within the project. Allied to this may be the publishing trend to have many authors on a paper, in which case it is possible that the local author does not get a copy of the final pre-publication text.

- *Discipline factors.* The fact that parts of our community already deposit in subject-based repositories, showing the strong link to the subject area rather than the organisation is discussed elsewhere.

- *What to do with bibliographic references which are not linked to CCLRC.* With an emphasis on populating ePubs with historic information we often get asked whether authors can put pre-CCLRC publications in. While this encourages input and usefulness to our authors, it does make the input and management of statistics more complicated.

Successful techniques

One of the most successful things we did was completely accidental: we put historic bibliographic records in. This meant that the pilot demonstrator had over 7,000 records in to start with. Being able to show the system with meaningful information in, especially as the records all related to one department, encouraged others to offer information. While this has meant that there is a low proportion of full-text works, it has had the benefit that authors can put all their publications in the repository.

Finding enthusiastic authors is another good way of increasing the take-up. Authors are often guided by peers. An important way of engaging with these is taking any opportunity to go out and talk about the institutional repository. In tandem with this, always being willing to give large or one-to-one training sessions on how to input material into ePubs and providing an effective support system for queries have proven beneficial.

The management team decided that the library and information service would offer to input historical data while encouraging authors to input current information. Not only has this increased the number of bibliographic records, authors enquire why only their older stuff is available!

Our institutional repository is run by a neutral party so that there are no departmental politics involved. The library and information service, although it has a place in the organisational structure, is considered to be non-political as it serves the entire organisation. This has avoided any potential issues around solutions seeming to be imposed by central IT departments. The library and information service has a good reputation for customer service, and ePubs benefits from this association.

The one tip you would recommend to others

Put your effort into the parts of the system which will mean most to your user community and then publicise this accordingly. For CCLRC this meant historic information and the ability to replicate the functions that were already happening, while transferring the support costs and maintenance to the library and information services.

Future direction

There are three main themes to the future direction: policy development, increased functionality and usage and research and development issues. ePubs has a lot of policy, but most of this is not available externally. We would like to use SHERPA OpenDOAR policy tools (*http://www .opendoar.org/*) to build more robust and visible OAI-PMH policies.

ePubs has been successful in many ways within the organisation, but we would like to continue to enhance ePubs and to encourage more staff to deposit the full texts of works in the repository. We are investigating publishers which allow retrospective input of full-text articles into repositories to be able to increase the content.

As a scientific organisation that produces data and also stores it on behalf of other institutions, the ability to link data to publications is an important development stream and we are part of the CLADDIER project (*http://claddier.badc.ac.uk/trac*) funded by JISC. We are also interested in the semantics of identifying copies of publications and will be investigating this further through a JISC project on version identification frameworks.

Cranfield University, UK

About the organisation – what does it do and what type of material is produced

Cranfield University was founded in 1946 as the College of Aeronautics; in 1969 as the Cranfield Institute of Technology it was granted university status and from 1992 has been known under its present name. It is a postgraduate-only institution, with three sites, and its subject expertise is in selected areas of engineering, applied science, manufacturing, management and medical science.

The mission statement for the institutional repository encapsulates the aims of many institutional repositories:

- To create and establish an electronic system that captures, preserves and communicates the intellectual output of Cranfield's faculty and researchers. Cranfield QUEprints will facilitate the distribution of Cranfield's digital works over the Web through a search and retrieval system and it will preserve these digital works over the long term.

- To provide access to the digital work of the whole institution through one interface.

- The aim is to increase visibility and impact of the university's research output, in relation specifically to e-prints, e-theses, technical reports and working papers.

The development of the institutional repository at Cranfield focuses on the desire to communicate intellectual output, and increase its visibility and impact.

The main types of material produced by Cranfield, and within the repository remit are journal articles, theses, technical reports, working papers, Decision Engineering Group reports and CVs.

What were the previous processes for material collection

Hyperion, a commercial digital library product, contained School of Management working papers, reports and some restricted access learning objects for a specific course. It also has a restricted access copy of a book from one of our senior academics. All freely available material was copied from Hyperion to QUEprints.

What was the impetus to start your institutional repository

In 2005 the thesis submission procedures were altered to make electronic submission mandatory, this meant that there had to be a system to manage and preserve the outputs. A project was set up to do this. It evaluated the three main alternatives at the time: Virginia Tech's ETD-db (*http://scholar .lib.vt.edu/ETD-db/*), Southampton University's GNU Eprints and MIT/Hewlett Packard's DSpace. DSpace was chosen as, at the time, it seemed to be the best resourced and thus supported system. ETD-db was also a specialist thesis system and this was felt to be a limitation over the long run.

Metadata was discussed early in the development of Cranfield QUEprints, in particular in the requirements for different types of material. As Cranfield was a member of the JISC/FAIR 'Electronic Theses' project (*http://www2 .rgu.ac.uk/library/e-theses.htm*) led by Robert Gordon University, the recommendations of this project and the later EThOS project (*http://www.ethos.ac.uk/*) have been adopted. It was accepted that records transferred from other systems (eg the library catalogue, Hyperion) would have metadata of an acceptable level from the legacy system and this might be lower than QUEprints.

The brand name of the repository took some iterations before the final version was decided. The initial name was CUE-prints – Cranfield University E-prints. After some advocacy with stakeholders it was discovered than the use of initials was not considered appropriate. The name was then changed to QUEprints which is phonetically identical, but this had the disadvantage that in an alphabetical list, it didn't appear under 'C' for Cranfield as might be expected. The final version is Cranfield QUEprints.

Brief description of the process

At present the content within Cranfield QUEprints is entirely mediated through library service staff. The project management team decided that the culture within Cranfield University was not ready for self-archiving and would not see the benefits, especially in an empty system, and so they decided to build the repository until it reached some critical mass, at which point active researchers would be encouraged to self-archive. The group that manages the repository reports to the library e-policy group.

Several approaches to gaining content, both retrospective and current have been used. Retrospective content has been identified and located through three main methods:

- *Uploading of CV content.* Information contained with CVs of staff associated with an intra-school body, the Institute for Safety, Risk and Reliability was uploaded to solve a particular problem, although the issue of updating these was not addressed.

- *Transferral of information from alternative systems.* The library used Sirsi's Hyperion digital media archive to hold electronic version of technical reports and working papers; these were transferred to Cranfield QUEprints.

- *Retrospective loading of specific publisher/author content.* The team identified two publishers that allowed the use of author's refereed e-prints in institutional repositories: Elsevier Science and Blackwell. These publishers were identified with information provided through the RoMEO website. The team contacted 25 Elsevier Science authors and 56 per cent of them provided articles. At the time, in 2004, Blackwell allowed the deposit of material as long as the author requested permission. The team supplied authors with a standard letter and more articles were retrieved as a result. The team also targeted important authors, who were likely to influence others to deposit. This has been extended to developing contacts with research offices with departments so that the library is sent relevant information as part of the process.

The library is now focusing on recently published material. Although some academics do send information to the library, the problem is to identify the rest. At present there are alerts set up in SCOPUS (*http://www.scopus.com/scopus/home.url*) to achieve this. Once the library is aware of the material, the relevant author is contacted to ask them to provide the relevant article. RoMEO is used to check the copyright position and if there is not an entry then the publisher is contacted directly.

There has been general publicity through internal newsletters and specific targeting of senior staff, both individually and through the committee structure. As part of the process, staff are alerted to the persistent URL provided by DSpace, enabling the library service to explain the aims and benefits of the institutional repository. This advocacy has been extended to library staff to ensure that they understand the benefits and can extol them to authors with whom they have contact. Usage monitoring has revealed that the most popular item has been used (as of December 2006) over 3,000 times and that the entire collection has had half a million views. It is the intention to use this usage information as part of the advocacy campaign to show how institutional repositories contribute to the dissemination process.

At present, spring 2007, there are now over 1,300 full-text articles. Over 44 months, the average deposition rate is 30 items per month.

Resourcing

The institutional repository has not attracted any additional resourcing to the library service. Instead, Cranfield Library has restructured staff roles to allow for library staff to add content by taking advantage of other changes in the information landscape, such as the reduction in handling print journals and the reduction in interlibrary loans as a result of full text becoming available due to large journals packages.

The recurrent spend and set-up costs were very reasonable at around £3,300 for the server and a negligible amount for publicity material. The main costs incurred are due to staff time, which has been reallocated within the library service. The equipment is housed and maintained by the central IT department.

Approach to curation of the material

Cranfield QUEprints is more concerned with access than preservation as most of the content is available from elsewhere. However, some of the Decision Engineering

Reports published by Cranfield are only available from the institutional repository and there is no paper version. The current solution is to ensure that all content is in PDF format. The management team will be dealing with curation issues as more e-only content is deposited.

Barriers and issues

- *Structure*. DSpace has a concept of communities and collections and it has been an interesting area to investigate the best way of setting this up. The current situation is that communities are based on the organisational structure, while the levels below are on formats of material. This can pose problems for inter-school bodies. The ideal is to be flexible about the structure. There is the issue of mirroring an internal structure when the external user base will not know or appreciate it; however, the route most users take is not through the structure of a particular repository but through a search engine. In addition, developments within the software are making this structural decision less hard and fast.

- *Subject indexing*. A recent decision has been made to include subject indexing in Cranfield QUEprints records. This will be available through a subject heading list. How this will impact on the resourcing and how the effectiveness will be ascertained are still under discussion.

- *Quality*. Although the quality of the content is not the responsibility of the library service and should not be contentious in regard of the type of material being added, there has been a request to be able to indicate refereed items.

- *Advocacy and institutional repository population*. Academics perceive that the deposit is time-consuming with no obvious benefits and there may be workflow problems or problems due to allegiance to their discipline rather than institution. Even if the author is happy to self-archive then the software may not be ideal in usability terms.

- *Policies.* The priority in the development of the system at the start of the process was to get a system up and available. The QUEprints management group felt that this priority was more important than the need to develop structured policies for all issues that may in the future be relevant for the institutional repository.

Successful techniques

Adding retrospective data and publicising the 1000th entry has made several academics interested in testing the self-archiving modules.

The one tip you would recommend to others

The set-up and development costs are minimal, so the advice would be to just go ahead and do it. Ensure your academics and researchers understand the key benefits of making research openly available.

Future

One future aim is to embed the process of acquiring research material into the subject liaison role, rather than as an entirely separate process, and to encourage self-deposit within the staff of Cranfield University. The Cranfield Library service has recently won JISC funding for the Embed project which will be looking into this area specifically, in collaboration with various Cranfield stakeholder departments, Robert Gordon University and Key Perspectives Ltd.

There is also more work to be done on the policy side of things.

The University of Otago, New Zealand

About the organisation – what does it do and what type of material is produced

The University of Otago was founded in 1869 as New Zealand's first university. The university has a presence in each of the four main cities of New Zealand – Auckland, Wellington, Christchurch and Dunedin, and will have over 20,000 students enrolled in 2007. The university is organised into four academic divisions and offers a range of programmes in commerce, health sciences, humanities and science. It has a core academic staff of more than 1,000, almost all of whom are actively engaged in research. The university is recognised as a world-class research institution with recognised strength in the biological sciences, anthropology, history and art history, geology, medicine, philosophy and psychology. There are nearly 4,000 postgraduate students on campus completing research degrees. The university has also earned a reputation for its entrepreneurial acumen and commercial energy, particularly in biotechnology.

Documentation of research outputs covers the gamut of digital and non-digital records that are conventionally held in the university and divisional libraries or by departments and individuals. The range of material is typical of what you would expect from a university: theses and dissertations, journal and conference articles, working/discussion papers and technical reports, books and book chapters. There is also significant content in the form of audiovisual material (e.g. video and audio recordings).

What were the previous processes for material collection

The university library has normally held research outputs that have been published in book or journal form. It has also held masters' and PhD theses that are required by regulation to be deposited in the library. Other theses and dissertations were held in departmental or divisional collections, as were working papers. Prior to the development of the repository, some collections were also available through departmental or individual websites, while other collections were not publicly available at all. The result was that there was no one single collection location or method of easy access for all research outputs produced across the university.

What was the impetus to start your institutional repository

The launch of the New Zealand Digital Strategy by the New Zealand government in May 2005 was the starting point for the interest in repositories at the University of Otago. One of the aims of this strategy is to ensure that 'New Zealand is a world leader in using information and technology to realize our economic, environmental, social and cultural goals'.[3] In conjunction with this, the National Library of New Zealand set up a working party to research the possibility of building a national repository.[4] The national library is working with institutions to aid take-up of repositories within research communities. In November 2005, following a US study tour to gain further insights into the topic, a pilot project focusing on the School of Business was initiated. This project had the following aims:

- To establish a proof of concept demonstrator for storing and providing open access to digital research publications in the School of Business.

- To evaluate the potential of the demonstrator for adoption by the wider University of Otago research community.

- To connect the School of Business with the global research community, in line with the feasibility study and recommended actions for a national repositories framework.

A project team with an eclectic range of skills was established. GNU Eprints was chosen as the software because it was open source, with a wide user base and good support available. There was also local experience of using this software. The project adopted a rapid prototyping approach which produced a tested pilot implementation ten days after the start of the project. This progress was made possible by the project brief 'to prove the concept' rather than establishing an institution-wide repository, which would have been a much larger and daunting task. The prototyping approach to development meant that technological, process and policy issues could be noted without delaying the project.

The project was overseen by a committee with representatives from the School of Business, information technology services and the university library.

The pilot was very successful, both from a technical and publicity point of view. As a result it became the official repository for the School of Business in May 2006 and is being considered as a model for the rest of the university. The proposal is for each academic division to have its own repository and for these to be federated and managed by the university library.

The pilot concentrated on material readily available within the School of Business, such as working/discussion papers, conference items, journal articles and theses in PDF format, which had no publisher copyright issues. Rapid population of the repository was possible as a consequence. An unexpected benefit has been the significant number of downloads of this type of material, ensuring a wider readership than previously.

The experience gained from developing the School of Business repository enabled the team to produce two specialist repositories in rapid succession. The first repository was created for Te Tumu, The School of Maori, Pacific and Indigenous Studies, to enable the dissemination of their research, including digital images and film of artefacts. The second repository was created for the rural community of Cardrona in Central Otago. This repository contains historical and heritage material relating to the community, including photographs, oral histories and historical records.

Brief description of the process

For the pilot and the production service a mediated approach has been taken by employing a member of staff within the School of Business. Their responsibilities include ongoing population of the repository and assisting with defining sustainable policies and procedures.

This person has been collecting dissertations and theses, mostly in hard copy, and scanning the title page, abstracts, acknowledgments and references. Her brief is to talk to the administrative and academic staff to locate those cabinets and shelves where research gems may otherwise remain 'hidden' or difficult to locate. When a PDF file is entered in the repository, a note is included asking that the author contact the EPrints Administrator granting permission to make the full text publicly available. At that stage they are asked if they hold an electronic final version of the dissertation or document concerned. Sometimes authors already have digital copies and this makes the process of entering material in the repository straightforward. To encourage individuals with hard copy only to make their work available, they are offered the incentive of a digital copy of their work, which has been well received.

Material has also been collected in an ad hoc way from both individuals and departments. However, one department has become accustomed to e-mailing their working papers as they become available.

The idea of a 'digital drop box', where researchers can simply 'post' material is currently being considered as a first step towards encouraging self-archiving. Hence, would-be depositors can submit their material, without having to worry about administrative processes such as 'filling in fields'. The deposits can be checked by a repository administrator or coordinator on a regular basis, who can then contact the researcher directly if they require further information. This process could be administered on a departmental basis.

Resourcing

There was no financial outlay for the pilot as the software was open source and spare hardware was available. Further to establishing the prototype, a part-time administrator was employed to assist with and coordinate further development.

Approach to curation of the material

Little has been done regarding curation, though there is an awareness that long-term preservation is an issue. The focus has been to collect and populate content that is readily available in the most convenient form (generally PDF). A backup system is in place to ensure that digital disasters are minimised.

Barriers and issues

- *Copyright.* In the first instance, researchers seemed to be most worried about copyright. Showing them SHERPA/RoMEO as a means of checking copyright status has helped to alleviate much of the uncertainty and with some history behind us now, copyright has become much less of an issue. The most significant barrier is deciding on what and how to enter extant material, especially work that is in tightly bound form. As yet, a cost-effective way of scanning bound material has not been identified.

- *Perceptions of repositories.* Individuals are not always convinced that a repository is any different from a web page, and consequently feel that there is no need for them to offer their material. The ability to easily track downloads for individual items using the provided statistics package has changed the minds of many of these people, and there are anecdotes of people regularly checking their download statistics to track the countries from which hits and downloads have been generated.

- *Content acquisition and timing.* Another major barrier is the lack of established policies and procedures, and particularly whether population of the repository should be voluntary or mandatory. This issue is likely to come to the fore in New Zealand with performance-based research funding, as it has implications for both individuals and institutions. If the process is voluntary, it can be time-consuming and difficult to track down extant material. This is particularly true for dissertations and theses that may be held by departments rather than centrally, or indeed by students who can be notoriously difficult to trace once they have graduated. Of course, this is an argument for having repositories in the first place, in addition to a mandatory policy on the submission of research outputs to make them visible and accessible.

- There is also the decision as to when the full text should be deposited and made publicly available. While it is good to suggest that the article should be deposited at the time that it is submitted, there has been a case where a deposited preprint was very heavily downloaded and then was rejected by the journal to which it was submitted, as it had been widely disseminated already and was no longer topical.

- *Statistics.* The response to the repository was very high in terms of downloads and traffic. Traffic was recorded from over 80 countries with a download rate of nearly 19,000 items over the first six months. Unfortunately this rate was out by a factor of five due to some undocumented assumptions within the statistics generation package which turned out to be invalid in this case. The repository statistics show that abstracts are viewed more often than full text is downloaded.

Preliminary investigation of statistics from similar repositories reveals the same pattern for some and the reverse for others. This finding warrants further research to identify what causes the variations.

Successful techniques

The following techniques have proven successful at Otago:

- seminars that demonstrate how the repository works;
- highlighting the statistics package to encourage interest and just a smidgen of competition between would-be depositors;
- encouraging key individuals to deposit some of their work and letting others know that the work is there;
- having an identified (and paid) 'repository person' who is on hand to answer questions and queries;
- not limiting the range of file formats, and reassuring individuals that file conversion is straightforward; and
- employing a motivated and effective management team.

The one tip you would recommend to others

Make the repository happen in your institution – they are low cost and easy to implement.[5,6]

Future direction

A proposal has been drafted for consideration by the library and university administration for adoption across the university using a federated model. The advantage of this model is that an institution-wide repository does not have to be implemented all at once; rather, individual divisions or departments can implement their own repositories in their own time. A sense of ownership encourages population and ongoing interest in developing the repository. Individual repositories can easily be plugged into federated architecture as the need arises. EPrints supports the Open Access Initiative Protocol for Metadata Harvesting (OAI-PMH), which makes it easy to set up a hierarchy of repositories that aggregate metadata from the 'lower' levels (in this case the individual departmental or divisional repositories). While the full text of items remains in the original repository, the federated repository provides the ability to search all repositories under its umbrella.

For the University of Otago, for example, the library could at any time set up a central repository to aggregate the metadata from all other repositories that fall under its mandate, including the extant School of Business and Te Tumu repositories. This arrangement would then provide a central access and search point for all repositories within the university.

A number of research projects have been stimulated by the development of the Otago repositories. These include:

- analysing and comparing download statistics from several repositories internationally in order to determine how and why some repositories are more popular than others;

- investigating the efficacy of institutional repositories in exposing their content to internet search engines such as Google;

- developing new techniques for visualising download statistics;

- contributing to the Open Access Repositories in New Zealand (OARiNZ) project, which aims to develop a network of New Zealand repositories (*http://www.oarinz .ac.nz/*);

- developing an easy-to-use installation and configuration interface for the EPrints repository software to enhance the adoption of this technology;

- engaging with communities to further develop the potential of digital repository technology for historical and heritage applications.

Comparisons

The three organisations support research communities but both universities also support students, the University of Otago also having undergraduates. There are overlaps in research areas between the three organisations. In particular, Cranfield University and Science and Technology Facilities Council overlap in engineering and parts of the applied sciences. Cranfield University and the University of Otago overlap in the areas of business and management.

All three repositories have adopted a mediated approach to gaining content but this is implemented in different ways. This is demonstrated by making library staff responsible for mediation in Cranfield QUEprints, while for ePubs there is a combination of mediation through library staff and trained administrators and at Otago it is done by a specialised member of staff within the School of Business. ePubs is the only repository of the three where there has been a low level of metadata input and full-text deposit by authors. As a result of these input differences there is more focus within the ePubs team in checking the quality of the input data as more of it has been done by less experienced metadata creators. All the repositories have been interested in gaining content to produce a 'critical mass' so that authors may become more motivated to self-deposit. Two of the three repositories mention author-related statistics as a motivating factor for other authors to deposit. Academic competition has a strong affect on behaviour, regardless of location.

All three organisations have concerns about ensuring the input workflow is smooth enough for end users to complete successfully. The 'digital drop' idea being considered by the University of Otago is interesting and I'm sure that is what many researchers at the Science and Technology Facility Council would like to be able to do too, although we have no plans to implement this at present.

An interesting difference is with respect to theses. Unlike both the universities, ePubs is not particularly focused on theses. One of the CCLRC technical reports series was designed for theses, but only one or two a year were actually produced as such. This approach to reissuing theses as a specialised technical report is a historical hangover from the days when most particle physics theses in the UK were reproduced as Rutherford Laboratory theses. As can be seen from the case study, however, the issue of theses and electronic ones in particular, was the starting point for the Cranfield University project.

In both the UK-based organisations, changes in the information environment, discussed at the start of this book, have affected the local library service delivery requirements so that it has been possible to redirect staff effort to provide the appropriate level of mediation without changing the staff levels or associated costs for the service.

Interestingly, national strategy has had more of an impact on the University of Otago than the UK-based institutions. This is probably because New Zealand is a more cohesive country and with a smaller academic base to work from, so there are more opportunities for agreement and common infrastructure. The University of Otago's repository is also newer in concept than the other two comparators and this may also affect the impact of national strategies.

In all three repositories the bulk of the present full-text content has come from material within the concept of 'grey literature' such as technical reports and working papers. This is an easy target to start with as there are usually internal processes to collect this and organisational support to disseminate it. There is also the issue that authors may be prepared to perform different workflows with this type of material than journal articles. This content decision has helped give access to this type of material to the wider world. All three repositories mention the importance of the SHERPA RoMEO website for checking the position on depositing the full text of articles from specific journals. This is an important resource for anyone who is concerned with the legality of deposited material.

The University of Otago's decision to federate repositories to produce a university-wide repository is an exciting development and it will be interesting to see if this produces more 'brand loyalty' in the authors of the different disciplines with a repository nearer to their academic structure. The additional repositories, such as Te Tumu, also highlight an issue which is becoming more important as repositories become more widespread and visible: what to do with content that does not fit the remit of the main institutional repository but the institution has an interest in collecting and disseminating. Te Tumu leverages the local expertise while maintaining a separate identity.

It is interesting to note that although all three repository management teams are aware of the curation issues, none of them have formal policies in place at the moment.

The barriers for ePubs are linked to different aspects of encouraging authors to deposit and, when they do, providing the right level of metadata in conjunction with the full text. This preoccupation is probably linked to the decision to allow authors to enter records from the beginning of the live system. There is also the issue of authors wishing to have a complete publication record in one system and thus wishing to enter records that are not linked to the work of CCLRC. This has not been fully resolved. At Cranfield University, there is overlap with the author deposit concerns, together with some local issues around the best way to structure the repository for effective retrieval. At the University of Otago, three of the four barriers and issues relate to authors and their behaviour and the final one is a problem with statistics collection which has since been resolved. These barriers and issues reinforce the fact the repositories are not complicated technically and that the most difficult stakeholder to influence to change behaviour is the author.

The successful techniques from all three case studies stress the importance of having content, and hence critical mass. They also highlight issues that are related to their institutions.

Looking at the top tips from the case studies, both the University of Otago and Cranfield University concur in saying that repositories are straightforward and so it is best to just get started. The other tip is to ensure that some, or all, of your stakeholders understand the benefits of repositories.

For all three organisations, regardless of where the original impetus for the repository has come from, the final production repository will be managed by the library service.

Conclusions

When I chose the three repositories for the case studies I was unaware that we all have adopted variations of the mediated approach to gaining content. In fact I was sure that I would discover that ePubs was the only repository with such a dependence on library staff and departmental administrators to gain content and that institutions elsewhere were full of keen researchers who were depositing full-text publications with beautiful metadata records. Now I discover, for the repositories I looked at, that this is not entirely true. I'm not sure whether to be relieved that my institution is no different from others or to wonder how the open access goal of authors self-depositing their research is ever going to come about. Our real-life experiences do not fit with research into author behaviour, where the majority of the respondents say that they are prepared to deposit their full text.[7] I wonder if this is the difference between the ideals one holds when filling in surveys and the tensions of real life? It reinforces the point that the barriers to repositories all lie in the cultural and behavioural issues rather than straightforward technical issues.

I was interested in seeing how others had implemented their local institution's needs in a repository and it was fascinating to learn how these very different institutions have very similar attitudes and experiences while implementing very different solutions. I have concluded that good project management with clear aims and a good communications strategy for the stakeholder groups are key to successful repositories.

These repositories all show the various benefits of investing time and effort into building these systems and the immense amount of extra visibility that they bring. The exciting anticipated developments make the future of repositories a bright one and I look forward to seeing what happens.

Notes

1. International Federation of Library Associations Working Group (1998) 'Functional Requirements for Bibliographic Records: Final Report', available at: *http://www.ifla .org/VII/s13/frbr/frbr.pdf* (accessed 10 April 2007).
2. Jones, C. M. and Mascord, M. (2005) 'Experiences of building an open access institutional repository in a UK scientific organisation' in Proceedings of the 9th DELOS Network of Excellence Thematic Workshop: Interoperability and Common Services, Heraklion, Crete, 11–13 May. Available at: *http://epubs.cclrc.ac.uk/work-details?w=33956* (accessed 18 June 2007).
3. New Zealand Government (2005), 'The digital strategy: creating our digital future', available at: *http://www.digital-strategy.govt.nz/* (accessed 10 April 2007).
4. Rankin, J. (2005), 'Institutional repositories for the research sector', National Library of New Zealand feasibility study, available at: *http://wiki.tertiary.govt.nz/~InstitutionalRepositories/ Main/ReportOfFindings* (accessed 10 April 2007).
5. Stanger, N. and McGregor, G. (2006) 'Hitting the ground running: Building New Zealand's first publicly available institutional repository', available at: *http://eprints.otago .ac.nz/274/* (accessed 10 April 2007).
6. Stanger, N. and McGregor, G. (2007) 'EPrints makes its mark', *OCLC Systems and Services: International Digital Library Perspectives*, 23(2), available at: *http://eprints.otago.ac.nz/565/* (accessed 10 April 2007).
7. Swan, A. and Brown, S. (2005) 'Open access archiving: an author study', available at: *http://www.keyperspectives.co.uk/ openaccessarchive/reports/Open%20Access%20II%20(author %20survey%20on%20self%20archiving)%202005.pdf* (accessed 10 April 2007).

7

Looking into the future

Introduction

All systems grow and change depending on the needs of their users. Some of this change is incremental, such as small modifications to enhance the way the system interacts, while some developments can be more revolutionary, reacting to changes in the environment or organisation. This chapter considers the potential for developments, both large and small, for the area of institutional repositories.

The chapter first takes our identified set of stakeholders as a starting point to identify areas for potential enhancements. End users of the information contained within institutional repositories need to be able to discover, locate and use this material, so future developments need to focus on ease of use and integrating repository content into their working environment. Tools will be developed to bring together content from the repositories by subject or to collect different types of content from different stages in the research or learning process. Repositories will need to integrate with other resources that are used for information discovery. The future for repository managers and libraries lies in developing tools to improve the administration and management of repositories and using the developing standards to provide a seamless information landscape. For depositors in particular the input process needs to be as straightforward as possible and to bring personal administrative benefits across their career. For information consumers, developments may help track the results of investment more effectively.

All these requirements can be generalised as different ways of linking and embedding the repository within the information landscape, both within and without the organisation. It is, of course, difficult to predict the future, so this chapter focuses on the near future.

Business process

For a system to truly be second nature to use – from an input point of view, it needs to be seamlessly embedded within the organisation's business process, for example, in the way it authorises and authenticates access to the statistics and reports that are produced. This is an area where many of the stakeholders' requirements intersect.

For the creators of information, the deposit process needs to be easy and bring further benefits. While such benefits can include wider dissemination of the work, more tangible benefits are also required. Using an institutional repository to hold information on works produced during an academic's career at a particular organisation may make career development and personal performance easier to identify and organise. However, few academics spend their entire career at one organisation, so there is the further issue of how a creator can keep their CV of publications up to date and be able to generate it from one place. The organisation keeps a record of its output so that even if the author is no longer at the institution, the information is valid. The new organisation will not want to enter previous publications in the main part of the institutional repository as this will distort their information and they are not likely to be able to have the full text for legal reasons. There is scope for developing a tool for managing publications based on repository rather than external bibliographic reference management software.

One interesting area for development is the concept of author identity – being able to programmatically disambiguate a particular reference to a name to the exact person whose name it is. This area is complex: names are not unique and people can change names and use many variants of their given names. Additional information is often used to uniquely identify a person. This might, for example, extend to affiliation, although this in turn implies the complexities of tracking their career. While some repositories attempt to do this for staff using local resources, there is the concept of achieving this on a wider scale by uniquely identifying different authors from a central registry of information. This concept is similar to name authority control within a library catalogue. In an ideal world, a service would be centrally provided so that institutional repositories could check that authors were not only identified within the organisation, but also in the wider world. The benefit of being able to identify people uniquely is that services as described above would function more effectively and cross-searching repositories would provide more accurate results. One of the many initiatives in the area of uniquely identifying authors is the Crossref Author ID Meeting.[1] The 2007 meeting brought together many experts in the field and they discussed some present initiatives. Privacy was one of the more high-profile issues, as the USA has stricter privacy laws than the UK and so answering questions such as 'what else has this author written' may cause legal problems. Although the CrossRef meeting brought together publishers and third-party information providers, this issue and the method of resolving it is of direct interest to repository managers.

For institutional repository managers, future developments focus on issues such as extensions to be able to support curation more effectively, and how to modify a system to adapt to changes in local and external working practices.

Some working practices, such as applying for grants, require information on past publications. It would be nice to think that this information need not be retyped but retrieved seamlessly from an institutional repository. To be able to do this, there needs to be some form of author disambiguation as described above.

One of the areas that can be difficult to track is who has funded particular pieces of work. While funders are usually acknowledged in the text of a piece of work, it is not always possible to do searches on aggregated services to be able to generate this information. Depending on the way that the repository is set up, then this type of information may become more visible.

Data transfer and interoperability

As most of the issues of repositories concern obtaining the content, there are several developments looking at more automated ways of getting data in and out of repository systems. The deposit advanced programmable interface (API) being identified is examining the functionality necessary to allow for automated deposit of content within a repository.[2] For the deposit interface it proposes that there should be a method of requesting a deposit, with the associated item for deposit, and that the process should return an indication of the success of the request and an identifier for the content in this new repository. This API would not necessary result in the item being immediately available within the repository; it might mean that the start of the ingest process has started and it is in a submission queue. There are many technical and cultural issues to overcome. The first is about being able to understand the content format and any packaging information. The content may be a complex object made up of many separate files but being one logical object. This must be presented in a way that the repository can understand and store while retaining the semantics and usability of the original. There are issues concerning intellectual property and rights. If the transfer is from one repository to another, has the original depositor given the repository permission to transfer the content to the other repository? What content validation and verification processes are in place to ensure that the content deposited is the same as the original?

Related to this is the issue of adopting standards and tools to enable the bulk transfer of material between different institutional repository systems. This is a more complicated task than just transferring metadata records and it needs to ensure that the provenance and fixity information required for curation is maintained, transferred and additional provenance information about the move generated. This might be achieved by the repeated use of the deposit API discussed above, however, it is likely that there would be a transformation phase beforehand to ensure that the semantic meaning of the metadata remained the same. This process would take the content and metadata from one system and migrate it to the metadata standards required by the system in which it is going. This type of approach is standard in the library catalogue world where MARC is used to interchange data between systems. There may, however, be some data tidying in the middle to ensure that local practice methods which may not use standard MARC fields can be transferred. This task is more complex for those repositories where the metadata standards are still developing as there is also the added complication of the content.

Another initiative is the OAI Object Reuse and Exchange (*http://www.openarchives.org/ore/*), which is examining the issues around discovering, linking, retrieving, aggregating and disaggregating and automatically processing compound digital objects to be able to achieve more object mobility and reuse. The compound object is made up of a series of discrete digital objects. These might include the metadata record and several different formats of the same intellectual content. This addresses many of the issues regarding versioning and linking similar items, as discussed in Chapter 4.

Automated metadata extraction

An obvious way of avoiding the problem of author reluctance to self-archiving due to the required metadata quality and completeness is by generating metadata records from the full text of deposited items. Most, if not all, of the basic information required about the item is contained within the text of the item itself. The obvious next step is to use technology to generate the basic information. However, performing this automatically is not always straightforward. Identifying the different elements of the document, such as title, author etc, is obvious to the human eye, which can take cues from layout, style and format. Doing this automatically requires these cues to be described logically. Different publishers have different styles and requirements, thus any system attempting automatic metadata creation needs to recognise these different styles. These systems can learn from experience, but it may take many thousands of documents to provide successful results.

There are several ways in which these issues may be mitigated. The present issues mostly concern the ability to find formatted text within a document. Changes in document technology may mean that in the future, key pieces of information may be identified by common standards so that other systems can use these metadata tags to locate information for reuse, especially if the documents are based on standards such as XML.

For author information and context there is the possibility of locating information associated with the user login to identify the name and perhaps organisational structure. This of course assumes that the author is the one inputting into the repository and that the user login information contains relevant information which maps to that required in the repository.

Any technology that tries to reinterpret documents is not likely to have a 100 per cent success rate. It is also difficult to know whether the technology would be fast enough to work in real time. It is likely that some of the information about the text and its context and the author will not be automatically deduced from the document and user login. As such, there will always be the need, at least in the near future, for some human intervention and checking.

Subject coding or tagging

There is a disjoint between retrieval methods used in the information resources provided in a more formal way through library and information services and Web 2.0 technologies. In formally provided resources, additional subject-related information is added by information professionals who understand the concepts behind adding subject information and have an awareness of thesauri or ontologies. In these areas, developers of the subject tool will have considered the appropriate term to use and how these defined terms interrelate. There will be preferred terms, synonyms, and more and less precise terms, as the thesaurus or ontology is a thought-out formal language defining an understood subject area. However, this tool is only as good as the person using it, and the information professional also needs to have detailed and up-to-date knowledge about the subject they are describing. This professional should then produce consistent terms over the field being described as they are applying a known world view. In Web 2.0 tools such as del.ico.us or Flickr, the users of the tool can add any descriptive word they choose; this may be more accurate, as they are describing something that they know well, and both the item being described and the term used have personal meaning. However, a particular concept may not be identified using the same term by the user community; indeed, the same term may have multiple meanings depending on the subject discipline and may not be used consistently by other people within the site. This activity is known as tagging rather than classification. Most systems that allow tagging also have tools to show the popular tags. Through prolonged use, terms for popular items usually go through a process by which everyone eventually migrates to the most commonly used term for that concept. This means that the information added is more accessible through widely used terms. The differences in these approaches are sometimes described as the difference between a tree structure and a heap of leaves. However, this tagging activity has not been in place for long enough to observe what happens to redundant or obsolete terms which are dealt with in thesauri in a structured fashion. One of the curation issues with tagging will be whether it will be possible to retrieve the semantic meaning in the future once the term is obsolete and formal thesaurus links are not present.

In the institutional repository area, most repositories allow the author to add keywords. These keywords may be chosen from a set list according to the formal thesaurus concept, or can be author-generated, which is just tagging by another name. There is evidence that many repository users prefer to do straightforward word or phrase retrieval rather than subject-based searches (although in the background this may well be using subject terms as part of the search mechanism). This is author-driven, unlike much Web 2.0 tagging, which is done by the users of the resource so that the item discovered can be relocated and used at a later date. Repositories may need to implement this type of technology at the user end to enhance take-up and reuse. While this may be possible for local users who log into the local repository, being able to tag resources across a wide number of repositories and have this information retained personally – creating a 'MyRepository' is a more complex undertaking. However, as Web 2.0 technologies gain force in people's personal lives, they may expect the same capabilities within formal resources as well.

Federated searching

Although having an institutional repository is very useful for the organisation, for an information user this may mean a landscape of isolated silos where the key to get in is not the information being searched for but some knowledge of the author or location of specialist subject centres. This is a similar concept to the researcher needing to know the journal publisher before being able to locate information when they do not know precisely what they are looking for or which publisher would be the best fit. Google Scholar and other general purpose location tools can presently be used to aid the situation, however, this is untenable in the long term and more sophisticated solutions are required.

One way forward is to look at federated or cross-repository searching. Such building tools sit on top of the repository landscape, using the specialist standards and common interfaces to provide extra functionality. As with the existing information resource landscape, there are many ways that the underlying information might be retrieved, for example, by subject area such as computing, or by geographic area such as Welsh theses, or by specialist groups such as SCONUL libraries, or by item type such as only journal articles. These are not independent of each other and the required information might be some combination of the above types. Some of these federations are easier to achieve than others. Fixed groups and geographical areas are more straightforward to identify and are likely to include fewer repositories, so management with some human intervention is possible. As discussed elsewhere in this chapter, it is difficult to build subject repositories from individual repositories without a lot of common ground and understanding of the subject concepts and terminology. This may be possible in small domain-specific areas but harder across the generalised nature of most repositories.

It is difficult to know how these federations would actually be made – would this be something that the repository manager chose to join, or something that third-party services would generate from the accessible information exposed by OAI-PMH? Effective service provision needs an understanding of what is being provided to whom and when the underlying services are likely to be unavailable. For a service to be continuously used, the context and contents need to be clear and it needs to be reliable, both in availability terms and in retrieval terms. Users will expect the content to grow over a period of time and that doing the same search later will bring additional information. If the underlying resources are not reliable, then this may bring changes in result sets.

The requirement for generating harvestable sets based on criteria which are semantically harder to define is linked to the issues of both subject access to the information and cross-searching. These are likely to be associated with a concept of domain knowledge which is open to interpretation and is of meaning to a small community of users. For example, deciding to expose a set which only contains doctoral theses is self-explanatory to most people who are likely to use it; deciding to expose a set of doctoral theses about materials science is likely to have fuzzy edges, where some experts might classify a particular entry as engineering rather than materials science. Overcoming this issue requires some formal ontology to map the different repositories' views of subjects. This could be done by analysing the full document rather than assigning keywords, but to be able to expose a meaningful set to third parties still needs an ontology to map the words located in the document to particular broader subject terms.

Overlay journals

Overlay journal is a term used to describe a way of generating the useful features of a journal if the journal publishing industry alters in a radical way. The model assumes that the traditional journal publishing mechanism is no longer the major way to disseminate information but instead authors put the final version of their article directly into an institutional repository, perhaps with no external refereeing. The overlay journal would gather together articles deposited in institutional repositories to a central point after adding value by quality controlling them, creating a virtual journal. In this way, the process of submitting to a journal is superseded by the concept of the journal trawling for useful content and then labelling it as of acceptable quality. This then links together subjects of interest to the reader and ensures some acknowledgment of quality. This addresses one of the problems of collecting information according to the location of the person who wrote it, which is not how end users think about a topic, and assumes a detailed knowledge of the researchers in the subject to be able to identify research centres. One of the reasons that journals are so successful is that each title has an identity linking it to a subject area and, in some cases, an approach to the subject area, for example, theoretical or experimental.

One of the problems of this approach is how the content would be identified. In publishing at present, the content creator approaches the journal with an understanding of the scope of the journal title. This could be replicated in an institutional repository world, with a link to the article being sent to the overlay journal. Approaching it from the other side, it would be a time-consuming business for an overlay journal to inspect all the potential repositories; on the other hand, automated approaches would have to be based on the content of the articles rather than subject coding unless everyone had adopted the same ontology and was using it in the same way.

Another way to achieve this is for the peer-review and subject identification to be done by a third party. With this model, the article creator would put their work in the repository and request that it be quality marked. The body conducting the quality control would give a quality mark if it was at an acceptable level, and could additionally indicate the subject field. These quality marks and subject identification could be used by overlay journals to locate the appropriate articles.

Overlay journals are interesting from a preservation point of view. If they do not actually have physical copies of the content, what longevity promises can they make? This may mean that as well as the subject and quality of the article, the journal may also make decisions about the quality of the repository and their curation plans. It is likely from a legal point of view that overlay journals would not be able to take a copy of the article – this would depend on the rights granted to the institutional repository by the depositor of the article.

Linking to research data

Many areas of research produce data from experiments to prove a theory. In these areas it is analysing the data and testing the theorem that provides the intellectual content of written scholarly work.

Using the word 'data' can imply that there is homogeneity about the content and production. This is misleading as the term can cover both a postgraduate student doing small-scale laboratory research or a large-scale collaborative project, such as the Large Hadron Collider at CERN which starts operating in late 2007 and will produce 15 petabytes of data a year. These differences in scale mean that some data is readily accessible to all as it is so expensive and complicated to collect, or is unrepeatable, or is in an area where researchers share their discoveries through the culture of the community. Other data, however, can be intensely private; in some instances data can be career-defining, while some areas are very sensitive to sharing results before publication, or have a different attitude to the difficulty, expense or ethical issues involved in collecting data. The Human Genome project decided that the outcomes of the project would be accessible to the community from the start and have been shared.[3] Many areas have data centres that specialise in keeping and curating information. In the UK, most of the Research Councils support this through the funding of data centres such as the UK Data Archive (*http://www.data-archive.ac.uk/*) and the Natural Environment Research Council Data Centres network (*http://www.nerc.ac.uk/research/sites/data/*. These data centres have access control for the data itself to limit access to the appropriate people, as defined by the funding body and the rights given by the data producer.

In this area, there is an inextricable link between the data itself and the literature describing the use of the data. If another researcher wishes to verify the results of an article, they need to be able to assess not only the dataset but use the same parameters and selections to ensure it is the same data. So, to be able to replicate small-scale experiments or to reanalyse large-scale ones, there needs to be links to the underlying data from the accessible literature. The literature will refer to portions of the data that support the theorem being tested; if someone else wants to replicate the results, it may not be possible to get the original test results and another experiment may not be possible. This situation is due to the scholarly dissemination process, conventions and the limitations of the print world. At present, producing data is not awarded intellectual credit in the same way as an article describing the production of the data and analysing it against the theory. One way to make this more accessible is to be able to link the formal publication back to the data that underlies it.

An important issue in this area is defining exactly what is it that someone would like to be able to link to. For collections of data made up of distinct individual items, such as a database holding chemical structures, it is easy enough to be able to refer to particular entities. This becomes more difficult in other areas. For example, the British Atmospheric Data Centre has a collection of readings from the Mesosphere-Stratosphere-Troposphere Radar at Aberystwyth dating over 15 years. A scientist is more likely to take a subset of this data than use it in its entirety. This subset will have a logical presence to the user, however, it may not map to the physical files containing this information in a straightforward way. For example, looking at some parameters over a longitudinal span may need segments of many physical files; however, the selection is still a logical entity in its own right.

To be able to refer or link to this logical entity entails some thought on the behalf of the data provider. If the relationship can be described as a reference, then does the data itself need to be 'published' in some form? What does applying the concept of publication mean in the data world? For the data which is kept in a formal data centre, there is the issue of how and what to keep. As described before, some types of data are collected over a long period and may be continually growing. Do versions of the data which have been cited in publications have to be kept as they were cited? If so, this can cause problems for versioning and even knowing that the data has been cited in the first place.

There are many projects looking in this area. Some, like CLADDIER (*http://claddier.badc.ac.uk/trac/*), are looking at the issues of publishing data and then citing both publications and literature. Others, such as eBank (*http://www.ukoln.ac.uk/projects/ebank-uk/*), have created a specialised data repository, eCrystals (*http://ecrystals.chem.soton.ac.uk/*), which has been designed to capture all the data resulting from an X-ray structure determination process in one record, enabling a researcher to reuse this and additionally capture stages that would not be preserved if the dissemination was entirely by journal article. This data has been made available but has not been explicitly formally quality-controlled and this mix shows the complexities of data publication. Borgman and her team[4] have done some research about the use of data in the context of digital libraries so that the resulting research outputs could be managed. The research concentrated on the data lifecycle and posed questions about the data produced, with whom the researchers were happy to share it, what policies for fair access to the data needed to be developed, and what tools and abstract models were needed to be able to use the generated data. This comes back to some of the OAIS concepts of designated community. To be able to link publications to the underlying data, the latter needs to be kept responsibly and for the same timeframe as the publication.

While the concept of linking publications to the data that produced the publication is simple and understandable, there are areas where this is still a complicated technical issue and will remain tantalisingly out of reach for some time to come.

In 2005, Microsoft formed the 2020 Science Group to look at the future of science over the next 15 years. One of the topics briefly discussed in their report was the issue of scientific publishing and the underlying data.[5] Aspects that were likely to change and improve scientific communication were identified as follows:

- data displayed in dissemination would be enhanced to provide a richer environment;
- provision of information could be dynamically personalised based on end users' needs and behaviour;

- links between data and journal article should be improved, and journals consisting just of peer-reviewed data may well be available by the end of the timeframe;
- discussion and dialogue will be transformed through the use of the social community aspects of Web 2.0 and digital discovery;
- technologies such as Open URL and DOIs could be expanded to enhance semantic discovery services where the search terms have use reasoning and logic so that finding something 'which does not agree with the premise of this paper' will be possible.

Key to the discussion within the 2020 report is that although scientific articles will not disappear, further and greater use of the underlying data will aid the scientific community to further discoveries.

Conclusions

As institutional repositories are embedded within the culture of the organisation and the individuals concerned, so the underlying technologies will adapt to changing needs. As the depositors and end users get more used to this information resource, it will be interesting to see how much of the technologies used in the more informal Web 2.0 services are adopted by institutional repositories. These repositories at present are mirroring the formal resources, such as Web of Knowledge, in the way that the searching interactions occur; however, in institutional repositories, the end users of the content and the creators and depositors of the content can be one and the same person, which is not true for current resources and it will be interesting to see how the tensions between ease of input and ease of retrieval are balanced over the long term. Technology offers some solutions to aid this.

Within the organisation and the associated business processes there is scope to enhance the usefulness and reduce the amount of rekeying, thus linking all stages of the research process.

Many of the features and functionality described here depend on the services having a certain level of trust in the repository, thus making the concept of certified repositories important for service delivery.

Notes

1. Bilder, G. (2007) 'CrossRef Author ID meeting', available at: *http://www.crossref.org/CrossTech/2007/02/crossref_author_id_meeting.html* (accessed 16 May 2007).
2. JISC (2007) 'Deposit API', available at: *http://www.ukoln.ac.uk/repositories/digirep/index/Deposit_API* (accessed 16 May 2007).
3. Human Genome Project (2006) 'Information', available at: *http://www.ornl.gov/sci/techresources/Human_Genome/home.shtml* (accessed 16 May 2007).
4. Borgman, C. L., Wallis, J. C. and Enyedy, N. (2006) 'Building digital libraries for scientific data: An exploratory study of data practices in habitat ecology', paper presented at the 10th European Conference on Research and Advanced Technology for Digital Libraries, Alicante, 17–22 September. *http://polaris.gseis.ucla.edu/cborgman/pubs/CBJWNE_REV_ECDL.PDF* (accessed 16 May 2007).
5. Microsoft (2005) 'Towards 2020 Science', available at: *http://research.microsoft.com/towards2020science/downloads.htm* (accessed 16 May 2007).

8

Conclusions

This book has looked at the issues surrounding the content and culture of building a repository. In this conclusion, the themes are drawn together.

In the introduction, there was a discussion about the meaning of the word *repository*, starting with a definition of the word, highlighting the aspects of storage and information discovery. These meanings encapsulate the purpose and remit of repositories. This was extended to consider how the definition is affected by emphasising the *institutional* aspects of repositories.

Few technical developments have been so strongly influenced by a community with such a sense of purpose as the open access community. This started out as a crusade by early adopters and is now becoming embedded in the psyche of active researchers. The open access principle is that the outputs of publicly-funded research should be freely available at the point of use. This can be achieved most effectively by depositing work in an open repository. For open access to be truly successful, it needs the support of a repository structure and a culture where authors consider depositing their work in a repository as the norm. This developing change in dissemination culture could be considered to be another facet of the changing information environment where the distinctions between information consumer and provider are blurring in the Web 2.0 world.

The perception of how the depositors and end user may interact with the repository goes hand in hand with other changes in the information environment. Developments in information technology over the last 40 years have revolutionised the way information is produced and used. The type, and even style, of information retrieved to support academic work may not have fundamentally changed, but the way it is located and used is worlds apart from the paper abstracts and indexes and printed material produced from typing pools. It has brought information production and consumption to the fingertips of the user. This change in technology has influenced the way that end users view the way they work. Particularly in the scientific domains, end users now assume that many if not all the resources they require will be available from their desktops. In the world of wikis, blogs and social networking sites, the blurring of professional and personal lives is most obvious. There is also an assumption that the best and most useful facilities in the social space will be available in the professional sphere. This change in attitude and culture needs to be reflected in the interactions of repository users. Repositories can be seen to be a bridge between formal and informal information resources, in that end users produce and populate the content, just as users of social sites do. It is important that this bridge gives the right look and feel to encourage its users to interact as well as they do with other informal resources.

Main themes

This book has revolved around an appreciation of the main stakeholders in the repository process and understanding what motivates them, together with the cultural and technical issues of achieving this. For the purposes of this book they were grouped into four main areas: the end user, the information providers, the mediators, and the meta-information users. An individual may fall into many of the groups depending on the role that they are holding at the time. Thus, depending on the role they are performing at the time, they may perceive the same issue from a different standpoint. An obvious example of this is the difference between the metadata requirements for refinement of searching, compared with the amount of effort, and hence metadata, the person making the deposit is prepared to enter. Stakeholders are a multi-layered set of people.

End users should be the main reason that the information is generated in the first place. These people may be interested pursuing further research, teaching and learning or just personal interest. Depending on their personal circumstances, such as their employer, educational institution or location in the world, end users may have very different experiences of accessing academic information. The increasing presence of full-text repositories is enabling access to this restricted information. At present, however, these silos of information, mostly using the organisation as the key, may not be as useful as other location resources. Developments at national and international levels should help to join up these resources and provide a more focused and satisfactory resource discovery environment.

Creators and providers of the information face different challenges. For the creators of the information, there is the process of getting the information into the repository and the dichotomy that the level of metadata required in the discovery phase is probably more detailed than the level the creator is willing to provide at the time of deposit. Finding ways and means to alleviate this is one of the technological areas under development. Tackling the cultural issues of changing behaviour, however, is more complex. The principle of open access challenges the current publishing model and publishers are responding to this by experimenting with open access publishing models. It is difficult to predict what the final publishing paradigm will be. This affects aggregators as well. However, the need for aggregator services does not go away. In the present information landscape, aggregators bring together information from different journals and enable cross-searching, usually by subject, topic or author. This functionality is still required in a landscape with repositories. Aggregators will need to be able to trust and assess the repositories that they are searching across in the same way that they do for the journals at the moment. While the publishing paradigm is being adjusted, the challenge for library and information services is as big as that for publishers. Providing access to the outputs of the academic process needs a particular set of skills and a well understood community. Institutional repositories are at the other end of the information chain and although many of the same skills are needed, the stakeholders in the process are different and they may not see the complementary nature of the repository.

For those stakeholders with a more tangential view on the information provision, such as funders and academic institutions, there should be some benefits from a higher profile to their input into the research process. It can be particularly difficult for funders to automatically identify outputs from their funding mechanisms as funding is usually mentioned in the acknowledgments, which are not always part of the metadata set. Some funding organisations are supporting subject-based repositories and other repositories are making the funding source more obvious. The institutions generating the publications should have a better understanding of the work done there and a good publicity and dissemination platform. However, this comes with responsibilities to ensure that the repository is resourced correctly, both from a staffing and technical point of view. The importance of peer reviewers to the academic publishing process is undiminished with the changes in the publishing paradigm, although the actual process is likely to change. National bodies, such as the UK's Joint Information Systems Committee, help to inform and support the stakeholders in this process. Principles and grand ideas such as open access do not live in a vacuum; successful operation of repositories needs organisational support and funding. For these new repositories to succeed and grow, the infrastructure needs to be in place, and recognised through certification processes.

All these different stakeholders influence the development of the repository within an institution. As such, their needs must be balanced to ensure a repository which is live and not just a burial place.

Any successful project or service needs to be managed effectively and in this context this includes both the technological infrastructure and the content. There needs to be a strong framework of policies to ensure the smooth running of the repository, covering both the infrastructure, content and the processes of the repository. Procedures and implementation decisions within the policy framework need to be well documented. This ensures that the system is auditable for good governance and can be supported over the longer term. The stakeholders in the project need to be identified and their needs assessed. An identifiable designated community and project remit helps to ensure that decisions about collection management and resource locator information are fit for purpose. These collection management decisions will inform the preservation decision-making process. For organisational take-up, especially for authors who may deposit material, much thought should be given to the approach to gaining content, and an understanding of the differences in approach for the disciplines the organisation supports is key. The initial choices of content are very important in generating usage of the repository and giving potential users a good first impression. The advocacy campaign should be built around an understanding of the stakeholders, choosing the approach with this knowledge. It is a good idea to start with the interested parties to build a firm base before turning to those who are not so interested in the concepts. An understanding of the needs of the designated community, including content creators, will help embed the use of the repository. Careful consideration of potential reuse will enable the best fit for metadata and representation information to be recorded.

Once the content and remit are identified, there must be consideration of the metadata to be used, with an awareness of both the common standards for data interchange and the internal uses which may require specialised metadata. The balance between internal effectiveness with rich metadata and being able to transfer records must be struck. As repositories are a relatively new field, the consensus about which fields should be present and how to define their semantics has not yet been reached, although there is work in this area. It is not so much the standard 'bibliographic' type descriptions, which have been taken from the existing library world, but the additional metadata required for the specifics of the internal processing of repositories which is still under development. Indeed, it may be that some of this is never standardised, as all repositories will have to adapt to local practices.

With the investment in the repository and the institutional usefulness, preservation of the content is an important issue to consider and this will become more important as repositories mature and grow. This specialist area needs specialised metadata to be able to ensure that this is successful. The Open Archival Information System provides a strong conceptual base for the services and methods required to be able preserve the content effectively over the long term. There is a variety of techniques to ensure that the data remains accessible and these, to a certain extent, are well understood. However, the trickier issues are about collection management decisions and whether there are enough resources to curate everything and, if not, defining the priority areas. There is potential for third parties to provide specialised preservation and curation services as many of the technical aspects of this are identical regardless of the content. It will be interesting to see what types of organisation decide this to be a worthwhile field.

One of the important concepts is that of trusted or certified repositories. As more repositories become available and populated then the issue of third-party use of the content will become more important. To be able to build effective and reliable information resources, there needs to be an understanding of what constitutes good repository management and the trusted repository work is useful in starting to create a common understanding. In countries such as the Netherlands and New Zealand, there are, or will be, federations of academic institutions. The success of this type of venture depends on the underlying repositories being well managed and supported.

Looking at the case studies, the UK-based institutions began developing their repositories subsequent to local issues that widened out to encompass open access issues; the repository based in New Zealand, however, was established pursuant to the national debate on the concept of open access repositories. At Cranfield University, the local issue of potential organisational change to mandate electronic deposit of theses and to define the management and preservation issues surrounding this resulted in the creation of Cranfield QuePrints. At CCLRC, the process was started off by the issue of performance indicators and the recognition that there was no one central location for publication information. In both UK cases, the remit now includes the academic work produced with the organisation. All three institutions recognise the need for the repository to have useful content before it can achieve great uptake from the author group within the organisation. The tricky issue of gaining self-deposited content from busy academics is being tackled by an approach which embeds the usefulness of the resource before affecting local behaviours. The high levels of mediation ensure that the quality of the metadata within the repository is good and that the information reflects the material type being described. All repositories have aspirations to encourage self-deposit, but the CCLRC/STFC repository is the only one with author deposit, albeit at a low level. All three systems have concentrated on depositing the full text of works which are internally generated, such as working papers or technical reports. These are low-hanging fruit from a copyright point of view. They are also institutionally important and are likely to be produced in a fully digital manner, leading to questions of resource location and curation. All of these example repositories have diverted or employed specialist staff to add and check content. In the UK-based repositories, these staff reside in the library service, and it has been possible to use this resource as a result of changing business processes within the library service. At present, the additional staffing resource at the University of Otago is with the Business School; however, the long-term aim is to have the university library perform this user support function. It was interesting to see how all three repositories, having been set up for different organisational reasons and using different software, had many features and issues in common.

Repository developments continue, together with changes in the information environment, and Chapter 7 highlighted some of the more important possible enhancements. Many of the enhancements discussed revolve around the use of technology to improve the interface between humans and software and reduce the effort required to deposit or retrieve information. This, in some ways, is easier to address than modifying the culture of the organisation to increase deposit. The issue of the relationship between the scholarly work and the underlying data, especially for domains which produce experimental data, is fascinating and complex. In some scientific disciplines there are wide-scale projects to ensure that the semantics of the data are understood by more than just the people doing the experiment so that the data can be reused by other subject specialists, especially in domains where the experiments may be unrepeatable. There are moves to make the production and management of the data as important and respected as the publication process. In this changing data environment, it is important to promote the links between the publication and underlying data, but at the same time, it is difficult to suggest how those links may be achieved.

The repository management community is vibrant, with many experts prepared to share their knowledge through conferences and mailing lists. This means that common goals and themes can be identified and worked on in a collaborative manner, leading to improvements for the entire community and its user population.

Conclusions

A repository is a long-term investment for the institution which, if resourced accordingly, will bring recognition and value to the output deposited within it. It is an exciting development in the information landscape. The users in the near future have different expectations for information availability and retrieval due to the internet developments of the last 15 years. The repository gives an opportunity to be more collaborative and active in the information dissemination world. It changes the interaction between user, creator and information resource, bringing the resource nearer to users. As open access gains pace and alters the information world in the near future, involvement in the management of the institutional repository gives library and information services a say and stake in how the information landscape changes. This gives professional librarians a chance to demonstrate their transferable skills in the areas of metadata and preservation.

Further reading

Allinson, J. (2007) 'Repository deposit service description', paper presented at Open Repositories, San Antonio, 23–27 January, available at: *http://www.ukoln.ac.uk/ukoln/staff/ j.allinson/or2007-deposit.pdf* (accessed 16 May 2007).

Caplan, P. (2006) 'Preservation metadata', in S. Ross and M. Day (eds) *DCC Digital Curation Manual*, available at: *http://www.dcc.ac.uk/resource/curation-manual/chapters/ preservation-metadata/* (accessed 20 April 2007).

Cohen, S., Naor, D., Ramati, L. and Reshef, P. (2006) 'Towards OAIS-based preservation aware storage', IBM Haifa Research Lab white paper, available at: *http://www.haifa.il.ibm.com/projects/storage/datastores/ papers/preservation_dataStores_white_paper-public.pdf* (accessed 20 April 2007).

Day, M. (1999) 'Metadata for digital preservation: an update' *Ariadne* 22, available at: *http://www.ariadne.ac .uk/issue22/metadata/* (accessed 20 April 2007).

Dewatripont, M., Ginsburgh, V., Legros, P., Walckiers, A., Devroey J-P., Dujardin, M., Vandooren, F., Dubois, P., Foncel, F., Ivaldi, M. and Heusse, M-D. (2006) 'Study on the economic and technical evolution of the scientific publications markets in Europe', available at: *http://ec .europa.eu/research/science-society/pdf/scientific-publication- study_en.pdf* (accessed 11 April 2007).

Electronic Publishing Ltd (2006) 'UK scholarly journals: 2006 baseline report', available at: *http://www.rin.ac .uk/data-scholarly-journals* (accessed 11 April 2007).

Heery, R. and Anderson, S. (2005) 'Digital repositories review', available at: *http://www.jisc.ac.uk/uploaded_ documents/digital-repositories-review-2005.pdf* (accessed 11 April 2007).

Jacobs, N. (ed.) *Open Access: Key Strategic, Technical and Economic Aspects*, Oxford: Chandos Publishing, 2006.

Jantz, R. and Giarlo, M. (2005) 'Architecture and technology for trusted digital repositories', *DLib* 11(6), available at: *http://www.dlib.org/dlib/june05/jantz/ 06jantz.html* (accessed 20 April 2007).

Jones, M. (2006) 'JISC briefing paper on e-journals: archiving and preservation', available at: *http://www.jisc .ac.uk/publications/publications/pub_ejournalspreservati onbp.aspx* (accessed 11 April 2007).

Owen M., Grant, L., Sayers, S. and Facer, K. (2006) 'Social software and learning', available at: *http://www.futurelab .org.uk/download/pdfs/research/opening_education/Social_ Software_report.pdf* (accessed 11 April 2007).

Pickton, M. J. and Barwick, J. (2006) 'A librarian's guide to institutional repositories', available at: *http://hdl.handle .net/2134/1122* (accessed 11 April 2007).

Rainie, L. (2007) '28% of online Americans have used the internet to tag content', interview with David Weinberger, available at: *http://www.pewinternet.org/pdfs/PIP_ Tagging.pdf* (accessed 11 April 2007).

Research Information Network (2007) 'Research and the scholarly process: towards strategic goals for public policy', available at: *http://www.rin.ac.uk/sc-statement* (accessed 11 April 2007).

Rowlands, I. and Nichols, D. (2005) 'New journal publishing models: an international survey of senior researchers', available at: *http://www.ucl.ac.uk/ciber/ ciber_2005_survey_final.pdf* (accessed 11 April 2007).

Sharing Object Under Repository Control with Everyone (SOURCE) (2006) 'The SOURCE project', available at: *http://www.source.bbk.ac.uk/* (accessed 16 May 2007).

SHERPA (2006) 'Advocacy', available at: *http://www.sherpa .ac.uk/guidance/advocacy.html* (accessed May 2007).

Swan, A. and Awre, C. (2006) 'Linking UK repositories: technical and organisational models to support user-oriented service across institutional and other digital repositories', available at: *http://www.jisc.ac.uk/uploaded_ documents/Linking_UK_repositories_report.pdf* and appendix *http://www.jisc.ac.uk/uploaded_documents/Linking_UK_ repositories_appendix.pdf* (accessed 16 May 2007).

Van Ballegooie, M. and Duff, W. (2006) 'Archival metadata', in S. Ross and M. Day (eds) *DCC Digital Curation Manual*, available at: *http://www.dcc.ac.uk/ resource/curation-manual/chapters/archival-metadata/ archival-metadata.html* (accessed 20 April 2007).

Van de Sompel, H., Lagoze, C., Bekaert, J., Liu, X., Payette, S. and Warner, S. (2006) 'An interoperable fabric for scholarly value chains', *DLib* 12(10), available at: *http://www.dlib.org/dlib/october06/vandesompel/10vand esompel.html* (accessed 16 May 2007).

Voss, R. (ed.) (2006) *Report of the Task Force on Open Access Publishing in Particle Physics*, Geneva: CERN, available at: *http://library.cern.ch/OATaskForce_public.pdf* (accessed 17 June 2007).

White, D. (2007) 'Results of the "Online Tool Use Survey" undertaken by the JISC funded SPIRE project', available at: *http://tallblog.conted.ox.ac.uk/wp-content/uploads/ 2007/03/survey-summary.pdf* (accessed 11 April 2007).

Index